Remaking modern fiction
ERNEST HEMINGWAY

Britannica Bookshelf—Great Lives for Young Americans

Remaking Modern Fiction

Ernest Hemingway

by Paul Rink

Illustrated by Robert Boehmer

Published by
ENCYCLOPAEDIA BRITANNICA PRESS, *Chicago*

Table of Contents

For Tina

Chapter 1

Beginnings

This is a story about a *man*. A man with probing, wary eyes, deep-set in an intelligent and mobile face. A great hulking barrel of a man who could move with the speed and the grace of a champion boxer, and the thunderous power of an elephant.

He was brave, and battle-proved. His body was laced and scarred with wounds from wars fought over half of Europe. He was a skilled sportsman. A 900-pound marlin he called one of his "babies." The walls of his home were lined with trophies of big game hunting. The great places of the world were his home. The people of the world, great and small, were his audience.

He was a man who could be incredibly gentle and compassionate. He was a soft touch for a sad story. A crying, lost kitten, a homeless animal of any kind was enough to melt him; and his house, wherever he lived, was filled with such objects of his tenderness. His life was overrun with visitors: his only requirements were that they be people of courage, people interested in doing something—anything—well.

He maintained an "emergency fund," available to friends in distress. He signed and personally guaranteed payment of $40,000 for ambulances destined for a people he loved, who were fighting a losing battle for freedom.

A little boy who yearned for a .22 rifle got the rifle, and was forever his adoring friend. Little girls loved to have him ruffle their hair and call them "child."

Like everyone, he wanted badly to be needed and liked and loved, and to have people approve of him. He was human, with all the nobility and beauty, and at the same time, the unpredictability of mankind. He could be tough, even cruel. If someone didn't agree with him, all too quickly his abrasive qualities would rub hard. He would excommunicate friends if he considered them overly wrong about something and if they insisted on being pushy about it. There was a code to living and to dying. In his eyes the worth of a man could be measured by the grace and spirit he showed when the going was rough. A man must live his life to the hilt and there must be no complaints if at times it was not easy. Life was an exciting adventure. Sometimes he likened it to a baseball game: "It is like being a third baseman and protesting because they hit line drives to you."

In addition, during all the fighting, the hunting, the fishing, the espousing of lost causes, this man found time to be something else. He was a writer. A very strange kind of a writer. He was a man who tried to write as he lived and believed, a man who tried to live as he wrote.

Was he a very *good* writer? Some people say he was up among the very best who ever lived. Others dismiss him by saying rather scornfully that any man who wrote and did all the wild, crazy, wonderful, passionate things he did really couldn't be much of a writer. He didn't conform to the popular idea of what a writer should be—quiet, thoughtful, pipe-smoking, a tweedy professorial type found on any campus.

Was he a good writer? That's really neither here nor there. The future can judge better. Some day his work will be considered calmly for what it is, rather than in the light reflected from the excitement-packed life of the man who wrote it. When that day comes, very likely people will count him among the champions. That's how Ernest Hemingway would like to be described.

For the moment it's enough to say that he influenced an entire generation of literary men—not just in America, but in Europe as well. His books and stories give a clear, truthful view of many, many things in this world. What he wrote has been read and loved by millions of people all over the earth. He won both the Pulitzer and the Nobel prizes.

Is it possible he was one of the *best* writers? Hemingway answered this one himself. "There is no order for good writers."

Ernest Hemingway was a man who grew to be a writer who grew to be a legend. What can be said about a legend? How can it be pinned down? Just when it seems he's fixed like a picture on a piece of photographic paper, he's gone and something entirely different shows. Hemingway was a man of infinite complexities and facets. Which was true? Perhaps all of them were and perhaps out of this has grown the legend.

Hemingway loved life and insisted on living it to the fullest. Unlike many writers who simply spy on life in order to write about it, Hemingway could only write about it by living it, tasting it, smelling it, feeling it. He needed to embrace it with all the strength he had and to let its essence soak deeply into his heart and spirit.

He said, "A writer's job is to tell the truth . . . My task

which I am trying to achieve is, by the power of the written word to make you hear, to make you feel—it is, before all, to make you *see*. That—and no more, and it is everything." Hemingway was the kind of a man who, in order to make his readers see, first had to live.

From this consuming need to live, the legend was born and nourished. Some say that even this was a pose. They say "the hair on his chest was false." They say that he really was a sham, a blustering fake, that he played a part like an actor on a stage in front of a gullible public.

Maybe the legend can be pinned down in the face of all the charges and countercharges. Legends must have a basis in truth even if it is slippery and evasive.

Even legends have background.

A man and a small boy tramped the open fields in the woods of the lake country in Michigan. Each carried a shotgun, the boy's nearly as long as he was tall.

A covey of quail whirred up from the brush, streaked toward safety. The boy raised his gun, tracked the flashing birds. He fired. The recoil nearly knocked him over. The birds all flew off. He had hit nothing.

"Ernest," said Doctor Hemingway, "you've got to lead the birds more. Remember what I told you. Don't aim right at 'em. By the time your shot gets there, they're further along. Aim in front of them."

"Yes, Papa," said the boy. His face was flushed, happy. He was dressed in old clothes; he was dirty and content.

Another covey of birds rose out of the brush. Up came Ernest's gun but before he could shoot, someone spoke behind them, a lady, a neighbor who was strolling by.

"You should be ashamed, Dr. Hemingway," she scolded. "Don't you know it's against the law to shoot the birds?"

Dr. Hemingway stared at her. Then he roared, "Never mind the law, Madam." He turned to Ernest. "Shoot the birds!"

Up came Ernest's gun. This time he also missed.

"Don't worry, son," said the older man. "You've got to have patience. Keep at it."

All his life Ernest Hemingway was to thank his father for teaching him how to shoot, to learn to match his skill and his own perseverance against those of the wild creatures.

Ernest's father taught him to shoot as a young boy.

The front room of the Hemingway house in Oak Park, Illinois, was huge—30 feet long. Across one end was a small, raised stage.

Little Ernest sat on the stage, a big cello balanced between his knees. He sawed away industriously with the bow. The sounds he produced were awful. He put down the bow, gazed doubtfully at his mother.

"Don't be discouraged, Ernest," she said, her eyes aglow with fervor. "You will learn how to play the cello. Through it you will enter the world of art and of beauty. You will learn of the world of the spirit."

Ernest's mother had a fine singing voice. She loved music and did her best to pass this love on to her son.

"I want you to promise me you'll practice hard," she said.

"Yes, Mama," said Ernest.

"Someday you'll be a concert cellist. A master of music. You won't forget this dream, will you?"

"No, Mama," said Ernest. He eyed the huge cello somewhat dubiously. It was nearly as big as he was.

Eventually he learned enough so he could take a very minor part in the impromptu chamber music groups his mother organized to play in the big music room.

Years later Ernest Hemingway was to say, "My mother kept me out of school a whole year to study music and counterpoint. She thought I had ability. . . . That cello—I played it worse than anyone on earth. Of course, that year I was out doing other things too."

Thus went the story of Ernest Hemingway's boyhood. His mother and father fought a constant battle for his heart and spirit. On one side was Mrs. Hemingway's highly feminine influence with its yearning toward refinement and the arts. On the other was the masculine, outdoor life that his father loved. The boy had ultimately to make a choice; it was to mark his life indelibly.

Oak Park, Illinois, sometimes called the "largest village in the world," was an upper middle class suburb, just west of Chicago. The prosperous Oak Parkers were proud of their wide, tree-arched streets, their big comfortable homes, their fine, churches and schools. Musical clubs, study clubs, travel clubs, literary clubs, civic improvement societies, and the like kept the pot of "culture" bubbling vigorously in Oak Park. In these, and in many other ways, the ladies of the town brought refinement and appreciation of the better things to themselves and their families.

Earthier, "depraved" souls were, of course, about, even in Oak Park. For them, the streets of nearby Chicago provided spicier, more pungent diversions. Rumors even ran that certain Oak Park citizens had succumbed to the enticements of brawling, wide-open Cicero, another nearby suburb, one which was to achieve everlasting fame as the stamping ground of Al Capone and other gangsters in the Roaring Twenties.

Ernest Miller Hemingway was born in Oak Park on July 21, 1899, the second child of a family that eventually included two boys and four girls. His father was a physician, Dr. Clarence Hemingway, a highly respected citizen. His mother, Grace Hall Hemingway, a native of Oak Park like her husband, was filled with overpowering yearnings toward the arts and gentility.

Mrs. Hemingway appears to have been a nervous woman,

given to "spells" and prostrations. In any family of six children, of course, there is bound to be a great deal of racket. Clashes of temperament are frequent. There is great need for understanding, backed by firm and steady discipline. When crises arose, Mrs. Hemingway's technique seems to have been to retire to her room upstairs with a sick headache and leave the problem to the man of the house. She dominated her long suffering husband.

The good doctor was a fine physician, completely mature and competent in his professional relationships, but uncertain in his home. He was the breadwinner in the family. He was the disciplinarian. He was the runner-of-errands. He was the arbiter of the most trivial family problems—the placater of his wife, the peacemaker between her and the children. He is certain to have changed more than his share of diapers and washed more than his quota of dishes.

In the summer when the family went to their cabin on Walloon Lake near the tip of the Lower Peninsula of Michigan, the doctor sweated out the packing and turmoil of getting them off. He got up to the lake when he could and in the meantime tended to his practice and put in his spare hours preserving pickles and weeding the garden. When they left Walloon to come home, the doctor invariably arrived to do the packing and cleaning before they departed. As the children got older, he spent much time and effort trying to keep peace between them and their mother—in person when he was with them and by letter when they were away.

In spite of his almost complete domestication, one part of the doctor remained free. He was a fine hunter and fisherman and loved the outdoors. Such physical activities seemed to him to be a part of the growing process for a boy and a requirement for real manhood. In spite of Mrs. Hemingway's ambitions for her son in the arts, and her yearnings for culture, the father did his best to inject his own loves into young Ernest.

When Ernest was three his father gave him a fishing rod. At eight the boy had his grandfather's Civil War pistol and marched joyously in the Oak Park 4th of July parades with the big weapon strapped to his hips. Then came a rifle and a bit later an honest-to-goodness shotgun.

In Oak Park people spoke politely. They were well-dressed, proper, formal. At Windemere as Mrs. Hemingway named their home on the lake, everything was different. There a boy could be dirty and go barefoot, could spend his days swimming, hunting, fishing. Summer time was for dreaming through long, endless, lonely and wonderful days—or for tramping or just lazing.

When Dr. Hemingway could get up to the lake, he spent much time with his son. From him Ernest learned a great deal in addition to handling a rod or a gun. He learned perseverance, patience, and above all, courage. Especially the kind of courage that drives a man to face up to what must be done, or to tackle the most difficult jobs against tremendous odds.

Ernest and he occasionally went deep into the woods on long pack trips. Visits to Indian camps particularly impressed the boy. The lives the Indians led, with the emphasis on homemaking and kindred crafts for the girls and physical skills and manly sports for the boys, seemed to him even at his young age to be normal.

To learn about Hemingway as a boy, it is necessary to study his fiction. In some of his early stories, there are intimate

[*17*]

glimpses into these trips with his father. On one such trip, the boy watched his father perform a Caesarean operation on an Ojibway woman to allow her baby to be born. The doctor had no anesthesia. He used a sharp jackknife for a scalpel and fishing leaders for sutures. Overhead, in the top bunk, deranged by his wife's long suffering, the Indian woman's husband slit his throat. In another story, Hemingway told how his father faced up to a terrible argument with an Indian sawyer. After threatening to knock the man's teeth out, the doctor went angrily back inside the cottage and started to clean his shotgun.

Trips and adventures such as these were very strong medicine for a growing and highly impressionable boy. They did much to develop his masculinity and to counteract the attitudes of his mother. His boy's life seasoned and hardened him, taught him powerfully the virtues that a man must have, developed in him honesty and integrity, and inculcated in him loves that remained with him as long as he lived.

He became an expert wing shot with his shotgun, a dead-eye with the rifle, and a canny angler for trout, bass, and pike in the lakes and rivers. His true bent was for the things that his father showed him. But he also tried to be a good son to his mother. In Oak Park he kept neat and clean. He was polite and proper. And he did his best with the hated cello.

He tried hard to please his mother, but . . .

One afternoon when Mrs. Hemingway was gone, the elegant music room echoed to sounds quite different from the strains usually heard there. Instead of the serenities of Bach or Mozart, there was the raucous clamor of strife, of combat. Grunts, heavy panting, the thump of leather on flesh, peremptory words of advice, urgings to more strenuous effort resounded. All the boys were concentrated on the action.

Ernest had turned the place into a temporary boxing arena. The size was just perfect. At the moment, it was complete to seconds equipped with sponges and water buckets in the corners, yelling encouragement at a couple of youngsters slugging it out in the middle of the room.

The sentinel posted for just such an emergency became too interested in what was going on and forgot his duties. Mrs. Hemingway swept into the room. With one withering glance she accused them, and crushed them. Then she vanished upstairs to await the arrival home of Dr. Hemingway.

The scene must have been a stormy one. Perhaps even more so when the doctor screwed up his courage and told her that Ernest wanted to take boxing lessons.

"Never," she said.

"But why not?"

"Boxing is a brutal, bloody sport. Imagine! Men hitting each other like beasts. Beating each other's brains out!"

"But it isn't that bad," said the doctor.

"It's worse. And besides, Ernest is to be a musician. A concert cellist."

"But you can't make him what he doesn't want to be. You can't make him what it isn't in him to be."

"He'll be hurt boxing. He'll injure his hands and his fingers and won't be able to hold a bow."

"Nonsense. Ernest is as strong as a horse. High time he is learning how to take care of himself. He's 14 years old."

Ernest *was* as strong as a horse. He was huge for his age, far larger than any of his schoolmates. The short bull neck, the massive shoulders, and barrel torso were already forming.

[*19*]

Mrs. Hemingway didn't give in without a struggle. She felt that her son was already spending far too much time outdoors hunting and fishing. He was spending less and less time with his cello and was neglecting his other studies. She had visions of him turning into a pugilist, a punch-drunk prizefighter.

The battle raged long and hard, but in the end Mrs. Hemingway seems figuratively to have thrown in the sponge and in a sense to have given up on her attempts to mold this strange son of hers into patterns he could not fit.

Ernest was enrolled in a gym in Chicago. His father paid for a series of boxing lessons. The boy climbed through the ropes into the ring, already feeling quite professional. He flexed his muscles, skipped a time or two, feinted and shadowboxed. This was the life!

"All right, kid, first lesson," said the promoter of the boxing school. Ernest's instructor climbed into the ring. He was Young A'Hearn, a tough, taut-muscled young professional light heavyweight in the pink of condition, in training for his next bout.

Ernest looked his instructor over a bit doubtfully. There was something in the eyes of the man. He squared away.

"Take it easy, A'Hearn," said the promoter.

A'Hearn grinned. "You're the boss. You know I always take it easy." He danced lightly up to Ernest, who also eagerly advanced for this first lesson.

There was a quick exchange of blows, a brief flurry of leather and flashing arms. Ernest saw stars. He was flat on his back, out cold, with his nose broken in three places. When he came to, the boxer said to him, "Tough luck kid. You'll learn

. . . sooner or later. This is the most important lesson."

More than a little shaken, Ernest staggered home to the sanctuary of Oak Park. "I expected it," he told a friend. "The minute I saw his eyes I knew what was going to happen."

"Were you scared?"

"Sure. That man could hit like a kicking mule."

"Then why did you get in the ring with him?"

"I wasn't *that* scared." Ernest looked seriously at his friend and shook his head. "No, I wasn't *that* scared."

Next day, to the considerable admiration of Young A'Hearn and his partner in the boxing school, Ernest showed up again with his nose striped with adhesive. He learned now how the "school" operated. Young A'Hearn was Lesson No. 1 for all students. The lesson invariably ended the same way. Very few of the boys returned for Lesson No. 2 or any subsequent instruction.

Everyone in the gym was amazed when Ernie came back.

Ernest stuck it out. He became a fine boxer. The kid from Oak Park was greatly admired by Young Ahearn and all the hangers-on around the gym. Over the next two years he collected a good many more bloody noses, loose teeth, and black eyes. In one fight the vision of his left eye was permanently impaired and that of his right eye seriously threatened. He developed a rough, but very much to the point philosophy.

When he returned from these boxing lessons, Ernest often entered the house by the back door and sneaked into his father's office for repairs before presenting himself to his mother. She was not fooled, however, and bitterly lamented that instead of a concert cellist she was going to have a punchy prizefighter on her hands before he was well into adolescence.

In addition to boxing, young Ernest also took part in high school athletics. If somewhat unenthusiastically, he played baseball, football, basketball, and went out for track. As he later said, "At Oak Park, if you could play football, you had to play it." He was big and strong and had no choice. During his high school football career, he collected more than his share of injuries, and twice during championship games had to be carried from the field.

Throughout Hemingway's entire life, whatever his exploits, he was always to receive plenty of publicity. His athletic adventures in high school were no exception. Since he was on the staff of the school paper, the *Trapeze*, he saw to it that his own activities were well covered.

He received one more priceless gift from Oak Park, exposure to a better than average high school education. Oak Parkers were rightfully proud of their school system. Salaries paid to teachers were extremely high; dedicated men and women were attracted to the school. The liberal arts were emphasized, and it was the boast of the town that four years at Oak Park High were the equal of two years at many colleges. Very possibly the proud citizens were right. The teaching was thorough and comprehensive.

When he had time from his hunting, fishing, and school athletics, Hemingway even at this age managed to write. Not only for the *Trapeze*, but for the school year book, the *Tabula*, as well as some things just for himself. His teachers and his classmates saw nothing precocious or unusual in this. Many youngsters loved to try to put down on paper their feelings and their reactions to the world about them. Hemingway's work was good for a student his age but nothing sensational. Certainly it showed little of the talent that was later to blossom. Certain traits do stand out. Simple, natural dialogue for one. Unerring accuracy in what he observed for another and a sly, tongue-in-the-cheek touch of irony and humor.

In spite of all the clubs and teams and extracurricular activities, young Ernest was essentially a lonely boy who tended toward rebellion and frustration. He had no dates with girls when in school. Classmates remember that he was awkward and ill at ease around them. In spite of his mother's efforts to arrange parties with nice girls for her son, he was pretty unenthusiastic.

Nor were the adults of Oak Park particularly interested in him, especially as a date for their daughters. He had a reputation for being wild and more than a little tough. Now and again he indulged in such highly suspect activities as sneaking off and boxing professionally, generally getting himself pretty badly mauled. Twice he ran away from home, accepting any job that came along—washing dishes, laboring, working as a farm hand.

These excursions never lasted long. He didn't like the idea of his mother worrying about him, and also he didn't want to fall too far behind in his school work.

Ernest did have friends, however, and in a certain way they tended to make him less than popular with the conservative parents of Oak Park. Like youngsters everywhere, these youngsters formed gangs of both boys and girls. Ernest was a leader of such groups. To the dismay of his parents and the shocked anger of the other mothers and fathers, Ernest often led his gang into the streets of Chicago and Cicero for a taste of forbidden life far removed from the gentler ways of Oak Park.

He *was* wild to a degree. Not however, as wild as many people have believed, or as has been written. He was wild enough however, to keep himself in continual hot water with his mother, with other parents, and finally, with his father.

Dr. Hemingway had his escapes from the tyrannies of his humdrum life. Hunting, fishing, an occasional trip into the backcountry satisfied him. Basically he was the reliable, hen-pecked husband and father. So far could he go toward independence, and no farther. Not so with his strapping son. Ernest was too grown-up for his age. He far outstripped his contemporaries. Sports and trying to date pleasant little Oak Park girls were not enough for him. Already he knew that life held many beautiful and tremendous and wonderful and sad things. He had to try them all, not just *hear* about them.

This his father could not understand. He could not understand the lack of discipline, the refusal of the boy to be molded and hammered and bent into the shapes that were acceptable. The father's reaction to living had been to bow to acceptability, and it had worked. If not perfectly, at least well enough to keep him healthy and more or less at one with himself and the world. Dr. Hemingway now fought bitterly with his son. In all truth, the father may have understood and sympathized with his son. Very likely many of their quarrels broke out because Ernest, in the arrogance of his youth, possibly had little consideration for his mother's views and ran headlong into his father as the older man tried to be the peacemaker and to make life "easier" for his wife.

By the time Ernest was graduated from high school, he was a proud, lonesome, rebellious boy. Despite the fact that he had eight full inches of "activities" in type after his name in the year book, and that his classmates paid him the compliment of saying that "None are to be found more clever than Ernie," he was bored stiff. He was bored with school, with Oak Park, with his family, with his friends. The taste for life was strong on his lips, and he impatiently yearned for its full savor.

The United States entered World War I in 1917, the same year Ernest was graduated. The senior class was presented its diplomas amid the usual music and platitudes. And then, almost in a body, the graduating boys marched to the nearest recruiting office to enlist. But because his father objected, Ernest was not with them. He was strong as a horse, big as a bull, and was a crack shot. When his father finally gave in, the Army doctors said his poor eyesight would prevent his being a proper soldier. He was turned down. Young Ahearn had seemingly taken care of Ernest Hemingway's chances at World War I many years before in the ring of the dusty Chicago gym.

That summer, rebellious, restless, his teeth on edge with frustration, Ernest went with the family to the cottage on the lake. Now, even the familiar tranquillity and the healing grace of life there failed to touch him. He was through playing at being a man. The simple act of graduation from high school was for him far more drastic in the changes it brought than it was for most boys. He was determined to be on his own.

The long shadows of danger and adventure that stretched all the way from the battlefields of France to the woods in Michigan claimed him. If he couldn't join up and be in the War, he could at least shake the dust of boyhood from his feet. In spite of the pleadings from his family, he wouldn't even consider college. He was going to learn by living, by clasping to his heart all that the great world had to offer.

He insisted. Something had to give.

Chapter 2

Apprenticeship

The long unhappy summer of 1917 drew to an end.

Ernest's restlessness became acute. His relationship with his father and mother worsened. By fall the situation was intolerable for all of them.

Ernest himself didn't know what he really wanted or where to turn. He only knew he couldn't stand things the way they were. He only knew he had to be free, to make or break his life himself. These were the big pretensions of full manhood, hardly to be taken seriously in an 18-year-old boy, but Ernest made his point. He announced simply that he was going away from the family for once and for all and be on his own. The future could bring what it might. He would be free.

To Dr. Hemingway's credit, he recognized that his son meant exactly what he said. Mrs. Hemingway's objections were overruled and the Doctor helped his son make definite plans for the future—plans that at least in part were acceptable to the seething youngster.

Since the excitement and the danger of the War were denied Ernest, he decided he'd settle for the thrills of newspaper work and become a reporter. In later years Hemingway said, "I wanted to work on the Kansas City *Star* because I thought it was the best paper in the United States."

Nobody on the *Star* would have disagreed with him, nor would very many of its readers. If the paper was not *the* best in the country, certainly in 1917 it was one of the half-dozen greatest papers in the United States.

Dr. Hemingway had connections in Kansas City. His younger brother Tyler was a socially prominent and influential businessman there. In addition, a trusted friend from the lake, Carl Edgar, lived in the city. Between the two of them—the brother to provide family authority, and the older, mature Edgar to offer proper guidance and counsel—Ernest might be expected to survive the dangers that lay ahead, whatever they were.

Tyler was able to land a job on the *Star* for his nephew. The family also arranged for Ernest to live with his uncle. Ernest kept the job on the *Star,* but almost immediately he moved out of Tyler's house. Ernest's idea of freedom didn't include living in a place where all his activities would be reported back to the family. He moved in with Carl Edgar, whom he liked very much.

Kansas City in 1917 and 1918 was a brawling, lusty Midwest metropolis, bursting with vigor and energy, coming apart at the seams with vitality. Vice, drunkeness, and corruption of all kinds were on every side. It seemed hardly the proper spot for a young Oak Parker to make an unsupervised debut in the world, but Ernest passed unscathed through the turmoil. The uninhibited life of a big city in full blast was nothing new to him. His forays into Chicago and Cicero; his experiences with bums and hangers-on of every description around prizefight rings had given him a worldliness far beyond his age. He simply added a year to his age, grew a big mustache, and took the city in full stride.

The city and his work were exciting. He enjoyed and learned from every aspect of both. Most important he was now exposed for the first time to something that was to shape his life forever. It was to indicate a path he would follow without deviation until the day of his death. This new thing was the magic of words.

He'd always been interested in words. Work on the school papers, and doing some small writing on his own had always given him pleasure. The *Star* however, was different. Here he was a professional. Here there was no fooling around. Here it was up to him to put down in black and white the exact facts and impressions of things he had seen in covering a story. And more than this, the writing of these facts and impressions had to be brief, to the point, clean, dramatic. He didn't know it, but he was being disciplined. He was developing what writers call "style."

The development of this style, forcibly imposed from the outside, became an absorbing interest. In the city room of the Kansas City *Star,* at the salary of $60 a month as a cub reporter, Hemingway started his apprenticeship as a writer. Here took place the painstaking beginnings of a molding process that was to determine the kind of a writer he would be the rest of his life. He took to it like a duck to water.

Pete Wellington, the assistant city editor of the *Star,* demanded much of his staff and he got it. A cub reporter had one month's probation to show what he could do. If the paper's demands were beyond a youngster's capabilities, he was sent

[*29*]

packing, regardless of influence.

The *Star* required that its reporters view man and all his activities—the foibles, the idiosyncrasies, accidents, tragedies, and joys—with curiosity and with a clear objective eye. Then it required that they write about these things in simple, dramatic prose. These two goals were "all" the *Star* required. They were everything.

So exacting was the *Star* that it preferred to take as reporters bright young men without experience and train them in its own ways. "We don't want men from big papers, and we don't want boomers who run around the country from one paper to another. We train our men, and we train them well."

To this end, the *Star* offered young Ernest Hemingway two extremely exciting journalistic traditions. The first was the famous Kansas City *Star* style sheet. Newcomers were expected to master its rules immediately. Hemingway himself later commented: "They gave you this [style sheet] to study when you went to work, and after that you were just as responsible for having learned it as after you've had the Articles of War read to you."

This style sheet was a long, galley-sized single page that was the *law* for *Star* reporters. It contained 110 rules which governed the writing in the paper. Hemingway in later years once said, "Those were the best rules I ever learned for the business of writing. I've never forgotten them. No man with any talent, who feels and writes truly about the things he is trying to say, can fail to write well if he abides by them."

The twin gods of the *Star* were accuracy and readability, and the style sheet spelled out how to go about achieving them.

[*30*]

The philosophy it proclaimed became Hemingway's own. It guided and governed every word he was to write.

"Use short sentences. Use short first paragraphs. Use vigorous English. Be positive, not negative." The wordiness and the youthful bombast that Hemingway brought from his high school writing withered under such stern discipline.

"Never use old slang. Slang to be enjoyable must be fresh. Avoid the use of adjectives, especially . . . extravagant ones."

Pete Wellington was the ideal boss. He was patient, dedicated, severe, untiring in his efforts to improve the paper. One might think that such a man, backed by such a clear-cut set of journalistic rules as the style sheet imposed, would have been a terror. Nothing was farther from the truth.

In Wellington's hands the style sheet became, rather than a rigidly constricting straitjacket, a goal toward which the staff could all aspire. The rules became a friendly set of guiding principles that helped the reporters assemble words into sentences, sentences into paragraphs, and paragraphs into clear and readable stories.

Within the dictates of the style sheet, very little was prohibited on the *Star*. Dialogue, something unheard of in newspaper reporting of the times, was encouraged, for example. The tale runs that as long as a reporter was accurate, he could write a story backwards if doing so made it more interesting!

Hemingway himself later said about Wellington, the "tough" boss, that he "was a stern disciplinarian, very just and very harsh, and I can never say properly how grateful I am to have worked under him."

The second journalistic tradition to which Hemingway

was exposed while on the *Star* was a man, Lionel Calhoun Moise. Wellington and his style sheet were stern, official. Moise was friendly and warm and understanding.

Moise belonged to a breed of newspapermen that has become as extinct as the passenger pigeon. He was the old-time, nomad newspaper man—a journalistic boomer. Although the *Star* frowned on boomers, Moise's stature was such that he was assured a job whenever he needed it.

Fantastically well read and travelled, Moise could be never anything less than an exciting companion, nor could he ever write less than exciting prose. From this man Hemingway soaked up the lore of newspaper work and absorbed the basic concepts of good newspaper writing. These concepts, like the rules of the style sheet, were to remain with him always. "Pure objective writing," Moise said, "is the only true form of storytelling. No stream of consciousness nonsense; no playing dumb observer one paragraph and God Almighty the next. In short, no tricks."

Moise was the idol of all the cub reporters, particularly Hemingway, who dogged his footsteps and spent hours sitting by Moise's cluttered desk listening to him impart the secrets of good writing. Moise was not selfish about helping a younger man; generously he passed on what he knew. Hemingway was an industrious and willing pupil. To be exposed to such a man at this period in his development was a fantastic piece of good luck.

He plunged into his work on the *Star* with tremendous energy. This surprised no one on the staff. Any youngster lucky enough to get a job on the paper worked as though his life depended on it.

[*32*]

Pete Wellington looked up at the youngster standing before his desk. "All right, Hem," he said, "here's your first assignment." Hemingway quivered with excitement. Cops, robbers, sin, thrills galore were just around the corner.

Wellington introduced him to a woman member of the staff, Frances Davis. "You and Frances will cover the Federal Building beat. Split it up, but I want you to go with her for a few days and learn the ropes."

"Yes, sir," said Hemingway. This sounded exciting.

On the way to the assignment, he asked his partner, "What happens at the Federal Building? What do we cover?"

"Oh . . . " she mused, looking sideways at Hemingway. She liked this handsome, eager young colt. Then she said wickedly, "O . . . lots of things. They probate wills. Let contracts for new buildings. Something's always happening around the post office. Lots of human interest stuff."

Hemingway felt his spirits nose-dive. "Is that all?" he asked glumly.

Frances Davis laughed outright and then she said softly, "What do you want to do, Hem?"

"I want to ride ambulances," he blurted.

She giggled, "Don't worry. You'll be riding ambulances soon enough. Cheer up."

Hemingway shared the Federal Building beat with her for just a few weeks and than wangled what he wanted.

Pete Wellington later recalled, "He liked action. When he was assigned to the General Hospital he had an irritating habit of riding off with the first ambulance to go to some kind of cutting scrape without letting the city desk know that he was leaving the post uncovered. . . . He always wanted to be on the scene himself. . . ."

Hemingway got plenty of action. He not only rode ambulances, but he finally was riding the police cars in his search for excitement. Wellington worked his reporters hard. He believed a reporter had to be there, to see for himself, if he was going to write well about anything. Hemingway couldn't have agreed more. Instinctively he was aware that the man who was on the scene, who "saw how it actually was," knows far more about a subject than the man "who just studies up on it."

The terror, the pathos, the sorrow and suffering, the ugliness and the beauty of a great city were his meat. He found them in the police cars, the ambulances, the receiving wards of the hospitals. During this period on the *Star* Hemingway probably covered very few civic improvement luncheons. His natural craving for excitement, his interest and love for the earthy, soul-wrenching, bloody aspects of human existence guided him then as they would throughout his entire life.

Hemingway not only worked hard at gathering material. He took enormous pains writing a story. He spent hours at his typewriter, assembling, tearing apart, reassembling words and ideas. He slowly came to be aware of the joy in putting down words that seemed to express clearly and briefly and dramatically the ideas he had in his mind. He began to know the thrill of discovering for himself that the English language could be made to yield to his efforts. He found that words—the great unwieldy, bulky means of communication that stands between the mind of one man and another—could be beaten and cudgeled and wheedled into obedience and be *forced* to express exact meanings. Each word was separate and independent and like a bright stubborn pebble in its own right; but they could be joined with others that came before, and after, and finally form a whole of incomparable efficiency and beauty.

The *Star* loved writers. There was scarcely a man on the staff who wasn't slaving away in private on stories, novels, or plays of his own. These men loved to talk writing. The atmosphere was tough and professional, but it was also literary. Occasional superior news-stories were quickly and generally approved.

During the seven months Hemingway was on the staff, he wrote a number of such stories. They startled Wellington and the others who worked with him by their power and maturity. Already the traits that were later to make Hem world-famous, were developing.

But in spite of the joy in his work and his growing belief that he was destined to be a writer and was being so molded, one dark cloud never left him. The War! Stimulating and exciting though the work on the paper might be, he could not help feeling it was unimportant compared to the experiences millions of young men in Europe were going through. The War was the "real stuff." Even though reporting was not make-believe, it seemed nevertheless a very anemic replica of what was happening across the ocean.

He never ceased trying to enlist and actually made application to 12 different branches of the Armed Services. Each time he was turned down. His eyes, so they said, were no good.

His belief that a man must be on the scene—must first see, do, and act, then write,—tortured him. Here he was, stuck in Kansas City, doing a fine job as a reporter, but obliged to sit helplessly while the most important thing that could happen to a man was going on in Europe without him!

[*35*]

One day he was pounding a typewriter, putting the final draft of a story down on paper. The typewriter was a very old one: the keys stuck and every tenth letter or so printed above the line. With his customary energy, Hemingway banged the machine, even though he became aware that someone was standing nearby, observing him. Finally he was done.

"That's rotten looking copy," Hemingway said apologetically. "When I get a little excited this —— type mill goes haywire on me."

Hemingway held out his hand. "My name's Hemingway.

Words poured out faster than the typewriter could take them.

Ernest Hemingway. You're a new man, aren't you?"

They shook. For Hemingway this was the beginning of an acquaintanceship that was to change his life. The new man was Ted Brumback, son of a wealthy and prominent Kansas City family.

Hemingway was astounded and his admiration for Brumback skyrocketed when he learned that though his new acquaintance had lost the sight of one eye in a golfing accident, he had managed to wangle his way into the War in Europe. Here was something of real interest!

Brumback had left Cornell University in his junior year and had enlisted with the American Field Service. He had served in France as an ambulance driver. When his enlistment was up, he had returned home, a glamorous veteran of the War. He had many things to tell Ernest Hemingway and Hemingway was interested in all of them. Here was a real veteran. He had been there. He had been discharged with honor from an elite unit attached to the Chasseurs Alpins. Brumback had done his part like a man; he had seen and known war.

"What was the name of that outfit?" asked Hemingway excitedly.

"The American Field Service. We drove ambulances."

"Did you see much of the actual fighting?"

"What do you think? Our job was right at the front lines. We had lots of casualties. When an artillery shell comes over it isn't particular where it lands. Sometimes we'd arrive at a field hospital and find we'd been driving a hearse instead of an ambulance."

Hemingway's eyes shone. He could hardly keep from stuttering. "And they don't care about your eyesight, or anything else?"

Brumback grunted. "If you can see enough to drive a car, that'll do it."

"Then what are we waiting for? Look Ted, let's sign up. Let's go over. Don't you want to go again?"

"Anything would be better than life here in Kansas City."

"Well?" demanded Hemingway.

"The American Field Service has folded. The Red Cross took over."

"All the same to me. We'll enlist in the Red Cross."

"Hem, I know how you feel, but it's no use. They're not taking anyone. All full up. I've been trying."

Brumback was right. The Red Cross was taking no more volunteers. Hemingway seemed doomed to fight the war from the city room of the Kansas City *Star*.

One day in April of 1918, Brumback and Hemingway were standing near the telegraph desk when a story came in telling of the needs of the Red Cross for ambulance drivers with the Italian army in Italy. The higher-ups thought it would be a good morale building stunt if Americans in uniform were to show up on this front.

The two young men looked at each other. They looked at the story. They couldn't care less about building up anybody's morale. All they were interested in was that drivers were going to be accepted.

Legend has it that their cabled applications were on the way even before the original story reached the linotype machine in the *Star's* composing room.

On April 30, of that year Brumback and Hemingway drew their last *Star* paychecks. With Carl Edgar, and another friend, Charlie Hopkins, they went to Michigan for a final fishing trip.

By May 12th they were in New York. A week later Hemingway and Brumback were in their lieutenants uniforms. The following week they marched 110 blocks through New York City to the Battery and embarkation. President and Mrs. Wilson were in the reviewing stand to receive the "eyes right" salute of the marching units.

The occasion was a delirious one for Ernest Hemingway. He seemed to be coming nearer to his goal. What this was he could not have told. How could he have truly known? He only felt that the trail to adventure and excitement had at last opened for him. This was enough.

From Oak Park to Kansas City he had taken with him a wealth of background material from an action-filled, joyous boyhood. He brought with him a zest for excitement and an abiding belief that he had to be "there," to see for himself whatever was going on.

In Kansas City he had added to the patterns of experience that were slowly etching themselves on his mind and his heart. In Kansas City too he had trained his eyes to see things the way they truly were, and to get at the essence below the surface. And in Kansas City, perhaps most important of all, he had taken lessons in writing. He had submitted to the disciplines necessary to forge the English language into the shapes and forms he wanted in order to express the ideas in his mind.

The great adventure had begun for Ernest Hemingway.

Chapter 3

Ciáo!

The tension about the departure of a troopship from port in wartime is quite unlike that surrounding any other human activity.

Last-minute supplies and munitions are winched aboard. Orders are tersely given, quickly executed. Men and equipment on the bridge and in the engine room are tested, screwed up to highest efficiency. Latest intelligence reports are received, scanned, and digested. The elements of danger and uncertainty are cut to the bone. Good-byes are brief and numbed. There is little to be said at this last moment. The wrenching departure is a thing to be gotten over with as quickly as possible.

Everything seems unreal, like those things in a dream remembered upon awakening—sharp and yet fuzzy around the edges, without true meaning or logic. One aspect of a departing troopship, however, is brutally real. Its implications are heartbreaking and inescapable, in crystal clear focus against the blurred background.

The loading troops. Like snakes the long lines of khaki-clad men coil slowly up the gangplanks. The parts of the snakes are composed of men, living men. They seem nameless, formless, shapeless pieces of humanity; and yet each piece is a man who moves before one's eyes as an individual, stumbling under his load of gear, utterly pathetic. The heads of the snakes vanish into the deep caverns of the ship. The shuffling tails renew themselves from the dim warehouse on the dock.

Nighttime, late in May, 1918. Lieutenant Ernest Hemingway of the American Red Cross climbed up the gangplank of the S. S. *Chicago,* an ancient and scarred veteran of innumerable Atlantic crossings. Hemingway was part of the scene around him. He was part of the departure of a troopship from home to distant and dangerous battlefields. He was fully aware of the tension and the drama. None of the poignancy and terror of the night was lost on him. His heart, his spirit, all his sensibilities reacted to what his eyes saw. This was ever true of Hemingway—as a child and as a man. He never just looked at life. He was always a participant.

Yet outwardly he reacted from the bravado of his 18 years. He was in the full flood of young manhood, bursting with vigor and romanticism. He was free at last of the shackles of his youth and family, from the nagging constrictions of Oak Park. Oak Park seemed almost a part of a life he had never lived.

The towering black hull of the *Chicago* seemed a magic vehicle to take him to distant danger and excitement. As he stepped onto the steel deck, he felt beneath his feet the life of the ship: the tremble of machinery, the vibrating hum of strength and power, the readiness, the blind drive to movement and action regardless of the consequences.

For Hemingway, the future held no darkness. He viewed it with no apprehension. He only asked that it yield him in full measure the exquisite joys he felt it must contain. For his own part, he would embrace whatever life brought him to the fullest, with no restraint.

The *Chicago* stood out to sea. With darkened lights she headed across the Atlantic, for Europe. Alas for impatient, young Lieutenant Hemingway. The passage was as uneventful and monotonous as the food and the eternal zigzagging.

Rumors of German U-boats operating underwater off the American coast had Hemingway and Brumback standing expectantly for long hours on deck, peering over the sea. Nothing happened. An unknown object resembling the conning tower of a submarine caused a quick thrill of excitement to sweep the ship. Later Brumback said, "Hemingway felt he'd been cheated" when the object turned out to be nothing more sinister than a forlorn barrel on a raft floating its solitary way across the Atlantic.

Hemingway was bored. Even the round-the-clock floating poker and crap games, permanent institutions on all troopships, failed to cheer him. The trip across the Atlantic he considered a failure in all respects.

When they finally docked and disembarked in France, Hemingway could hardly restrain himself. He was grimly determined to find this war he'd heard so much about and have a part in it. As quickly as possible. Paris was a little better than the humdrum routine of life on the *Chicago*. Not much better, perhaps, but certainly an improvement. When he and Brumback detrained at the Gare du Nord, the city was in the middle of heavy shelling by Big Bertha, Germany's latest long-range cannon.

Hemingway knew no French, but Brumback spoke the language. Hemingway commandeered a taxi and ordered Brum-

[*42*]

back to "tell the taxi to drive where those shells are falling," meantime shoving franc notes at the astonished driver. "We'll get a story for the *Star* that'll make their eyes pop out back in Kansas City."

Then began one of the weirdest and wildest taxi rides in the history of Paris—and Paris is not noted for its sedate taxi rides! For an hour they raced through the city trying to catch up with the shell bursts. The pair was lucky the race didn't end in a draw, but it was close. They actually predicted the course of one shell and managed to be nearby when it landed.

"The shell hit the facade of the Madeleine," Brumback later wrote, "chipping off a foot or so of stone." Then he added in perfect *Star* style, right out of Pete Wellington's style sheet: "No one was hurt. We heard the projectile rush overhead. It sounded as if it were going to land right in the taxi with us. It was quite exciting."

Eventually, chasing Big Bertha shells about Paris became as monotonous as scanning the greasy swells of the Atlantic had been on the *Chicago*.

Hemingway and Brumback made the rounds of the restaurants, the music halls, and the bistros, but this pursuit too, very quickly bored them. "I could find more excitement of this kind back in Kansas City or Chicago," grumbled Hemingway. "The war's going to be over before I've seen any of it."

Not quite. A few days later he and Brumback left for Italy, for Milan. Soon, like any excited tourist, Hemingway was sending postcards back to Kansas City. "Having a wonderful time!!! Had my baptism of fire my first day here, when an entire munitions plant exploded. We carried them in like at the General Hospital, Kansas City."

[*43*]

This amazing reaction to the horrors and the human suffering brought about by the explosion of an entire munitions plant sounds like something that might have been written by a cross between a six-year-old child and an inhuman robot. This judgment, however, is too easy. Hemingway has always been a very complex man, a man of many, many facets. There has always been a public Hemingway. Even at 18 there was a rough, tough public image of Hemingway—beating his chest one moment, spilling tears of sentiment the next, filled with bravado, thirsting for gore. Inside, there was another individual, fully aware of the pain, or the sorrow, in any given situation. This hidden personality never stopped recording events for future use, never stopped squeezing the last drop of significance and compassion from them.

"Having a wonderful time!!!" said his postcard. The only thing missing was the cliché "wish you were here" to match the cliché of "baptism of fire." On his own heart the episode of the munitions plant burned other words. Fourteen years later he wrote, bitterly, angrily, in an antiwar story, "A Natural History of the Dead": "Regarding the sex of the dead, it is a fact that one becomes so accustomed to the sight of all the dead being men that the sight of a dead woman is quite shocking. I first saw inversion of the usual sex of the dead after the explosion of a munition factory which had been situated in the countryside near Milan. . . . I remember that after we had searched quite thoroughly for the complete dead we collected fragments." But this was 14 years later. Now, at the front in Italy, Hemingway's main concern after this first "baptism" was to find more of the fighting. In Italy, in 1918, the front was never far away. From Milan, Hemingway's outfit was shipped to Schio, some hundred miles distant. Before leaving for this new assignment, Hemingway got off another enthusiastic letter for his public: "I go to the front tomorrow. Oh Boy!!! I'm glad I'm in it!"

Up to this time the Italians and the Austrians by mutual consent had not bombarded certain towns. Schio was one of these. The Austrians, however, had just violated the pledge, and so there was plenty of work in Schio for the ambulance unit.

In addition to the excitement of these bombardments, there was in Schio another attraction for Hemingway. From its headquarters in Rome the American Red Cross issued a steady stream of reports, bulletins and communiques. Hemingway's unit, No. IV, decided that even more were needed; so it published its own newspaper. The name of the paper was *CIAO!*, which in Italian, means "so long." The paper, about on a level of a mediocre high school publication, asked its readers for contributions. Hemingway needed no second invitation. The story he contributed was the longest piece in the paper, over 800 words. It brought a touch of hard, professional competence to an otherwise quite amateurish publication. "Al Receives Another Letter" was sharp, sardonic, to the point. It was coherent, expertly organized and reflected in every word not only the crystal-hard discipline of the *Star,* but the talent of the writer as well.

In his own mind, Hemingway was already a writer and this story in *CIAO!* confirmed the opinion in others as well. Its publication established Hemingway very firmly as a writer in the sight of his companions. They remembered him and the story long afterwards. They recalled the very evident delight he got during the time he was writing it.

In this period he also wrote a number of short stories. Some he sent to a friend in the United States, who submitted them to various publications. Regularly they were rejected— the first of the many rejection slips Hemingway was to harvest over the years.

But he had not come to Italy to write. He'd come to take part in a war and soon was grumbling his head off that Schio was a country club, where nothing ever happened. In spite of the artillery bombardments, Schio was not the front. The growling of the *real war,* as Hemingway considered that of the front lines to be, was audible just beyond the hills. He longed to be in it. He was disgusted with the secondary part he was playing. A drama of life and death ebbed and flooded nearby. A vital struggle for a way of life, for freedom, surged almost within the limits of his vision. A real *man* belonged there. Or so Ernest Hemingway told himself in that bloody year of 1918. He very seriously considered getting out of the Ambulance Service entirely and volunteering with a combat outfit for duty along the Piave River front. "They play ball down there," he grimly told his public back in the United States.

Things looked up when he was detailed to drive a Fiat attached to an Italian unit. For a brief time this duty in the mountains satisfied him, but soon his warlike ambitions caused him to tire of such unmilitary activities. He became increasingly itchy; he yearned to be where the glory was, where the guns rumbled, with the fighting men and the action.

Characteristically, he solved his own problem. He left the Ambulance Service but still stayed with the Red Cross. He wangled his way into duty with the canteens along the front of the Piave River. At the moment he arrived, the Italians were in the midst of a big counteroffensive. Soon he was in the middle of all the action and excitement he could hope for. Of the 17 canteens located along the front, some were in the mountains, some in flat lands; but all of them were within a mile or two of the actual fighting lines. Every few days the soldiers in the trenches were allowed to retire briefly to the canteens to write letters home and to rest a bit. The canteens were within easy range of Austrian shellfire; many of the huts were hit and demolished. Occasionally men serving in them were wounded. Just before Hemingway arrived on his new assignment, an American Red Cross lieutenant had been killed in a shelling. At last, thought Hemingway, things were looking up. If he wasn't in actual combat, he was certainly awfully close.

After a few days of supervising the pouring of coffee and passing out of candy bars, postcards, and cigarettes to the weary men from the trenches, Hemingway again was fed up and bored. Awfully close was not close enough! He had made friends with many Italian combat officers. Now he persuaded them that he could improve morale and serve democracy better by delivering his wares more directly. Accordingly each day he mounted a bicycle and delivered them straight to the men on duty in the trenches.

Hemingway became a familiar and welcome sight. *Giovane Americano*—the young American—as the Italians called him, balked at nothing. For six days he continued this highly dangerous activity. In those six days he soaked up enough of the sorrow and agony and realism of the trenches to last a lifetime. As always with Ernest Hemingway, he presented to the outside world the tough, flamboyant, adventure seeking exterior. Within, his mind worked at lightning speed, recording all the sensations—sensations and emotions enough to form the highly accurate background for fine stories and novels later on.

Quickly the artist was being shaped—and consciously shaping itself in the life about him. Of this period, he later said, "I learned about people under stress, and before and after it." "Also," he added wryly, "I learned considerable about myself." His sharp eyes missed nothing. They saw "how it was" with the gloss that hides the truth all worn away. He learned how men endured their lives in the trenches right on the scene, not from studying up on it.

The Italian soldiers considered that *giovane Americano* led a charmed life. The illusion was shattered, literally, at midnight on July 8—two weeks before his 19th birthdate. Many legends and stories have arisen about what happened. Some say that Hemingway was firing at enemy positions with a rifle and thus betrayed his location to the Austrian gunners. Others say that he had crawled out into no-man's-land to rescue a wounded Italian sniper. The truth is exciting enough without embellishment of any kind.

A huge Austrian trench mortar firing a projectile called an "ash can" because of its approximate size and shape zeroed in on Hemingway's position. The ash can exploded near him and three Italian soldiers. One of them was killed outright. Another had both legs blown off. The third was very seriously wounded. Hemingway was peppered by shrapnel and knocked out.

When he came to, he loaded the wounded man on his back and began the long, tortuous trip to a first-aid dugout.

[48]

Hemingway bore his burden grimly to the first-aid dugout.

Enemy gunners spotted them and a heavy machine-gun battery opened fire. Yard by yard Hemingway struggled through the mud toward safety. To the ghastly din and noise of the firing were added the agonized cries of the wounded man he carried.

As he staggered his way along the slippery riverbank, the machine-gun bullets found their target. The wounded man was killed. At the time Hemingway didn't even know the man had died. One of the bullets hit and tore into Hemingway's knee. Another smacked into his ankle. Later he was to write his family: "My feet felt like I had rubber boots full of water on (hot water), and my knee cap was acting queer. The machine gun bullet felt just like a sharp smack on the leg with an icy snowball."

At last he neared the safety of the first-aid dugout. Hands reached up to the parapet to help him in. As the Italians unloaded the inert form from his shoulders, Hemingway passed out. When he came to he was on a stretcher being carried to a medical station several miles to the rear. The road was under bombardment by the Austrians. Each time a shell came whistling over and landed nearby, the stretcher-bearers dropped him abruptly on the road and dived for cover. This happened more than once on the long, pain-wracked journey. The trip was a horrible nightmare that Hemingway was never to forget.

When they arrived at the dressing station, they found it had been evacuated. Hemingway was forced to lie in a stable during the bombardment for over two hours. Finally an ambulance arrived and took him to still another field hospital.

Hemingway's body was punctured like a sieve by shrapnel. The doctors counted 237 holes! They removed 28 of the worst fragments—devilish bits of steel rod sawed into half-inch long pieces. Five days went by before he was strong enough to be moved to a hospital in Milan. There the total number of pieces of shrapnel removed rose to 180! For him to be alive at all was miraculous. Years later, pieces of shrapnel the surgeons never found still worked their way through his body, bothering him when the weather was very hot or cold.

So Hemingway had his war experiences. His knowledge of life and the world had increased enormously, as had his own insight. But as usual, he paid a high price. In addition to the shrapnel wounds, one kneecap had been permanently destroyed by the machine-gun bullet and was replaced by an aluminum one. Only after 12 operations, including a bone graft on his ankle, was he reasonably fit again.

For his heroism he was recommended for the *Croce de Guerra* with three citations and the *Medaglia d'Argento de Valore Militare,* Italy's next to highest military decoration. It entitled him to a lifetime pension of about $50 a year.

During the painful months of recovery in the hospital, Hemingway had a great deal of time to think and to digest what he had seen and learned at the front. In a very real sense, this was a time of farewell, of *Ciáo!* to boyhood. Scarcely 19, he was nearly as mature as a man. The background of experience forming a part of his literary apprenticeship was also nearly complete.

He had faced death squarely and forever after was to live on easy, but fascinated terms with it. He had got his own protective talisman from a young English officer in the hospital with him, who quoted from Shakespeare's *Henry IV*: "By my troth I care not; a man can die but once; we owe God a death . . . and let it go which way it will, he that does this year is quit for the next."

Years later some were to say that Hemingway was hardboiled. They were to brand him as merely a callous recorder of the bloody and violent. They were to accept the casual easy judgment of his public image. Of this, he was to say, "I have not been at all hardboiled since July 8, 1918—on the night of which I discovered that that also was vanity."

Far more than Hemingway's legs had been shattered on that agonized trek back from the trenches near Fossalta, the little village on the Piave River. Many of his dreams, his illusions too, fell victim to the shrapnel of the Austrian mortar and to the machine-gun bullets.

He summed it up later: "When you go to war as a boy you have a great illusion of immortality. Other people get killed; not you. . . . Then when you are badly wounded the first time you lose that illusion and you know it can happen to you. After being severely wounded . . . I had a bad time until I figured it out that nothing could happen to me that had not happened to all men before me. Whatever I had to do men had always done."

These words he wrote many years later to his own son when the boy took up arms and marched off to another war. From a father they were words indeed to hearten a young man. Not sloppy sentimentality that would wither in time of need, they expressed rather the beauty and the strength of what was true. The words looked the terror squarely in the face. From their honesty would come the comfort a man would need to sustain him in crisis when the going was rough. But this was all in years to come. As always with Hemingway, experiences

[52]

required time to settle, to jell, to be evaluated truly.

While still in the hospital, he fell in love, desperately, head over heels in love with his young nurse. She returned his affection. The time was an extremely happy one for the wounded young soldier and he made great plans for the future. Alas! When Hemingway returned to the United States she wrote that she was going to marry an older, more mature man. A bitter pill indeed.

Meantime, the war was still struggling on to its final crimson end and to release for humanity. Dutifully he reported through his friend Brumback to the family in far-off Oak Park. "I intend to stick to ambulance driving from now on."

Scarcely were the words out of his mouth when he was discharged from the hospital. He wangled an assignment in the regular Italian infantry. *Giovane Americano* was very welcome. There was no question about his supposedly bad eyes. He served with the crack Arditi regiment as a bona fide fighting infantryman until the Armistice in November, 1918. He was discharged by the Red Cross on January 4, 1919, and a few days later sailed for home on the liner *Guiseppe Verdi*.

One war was over for Ernest Hemingway, but there were more to come—a fact unexpected in those euphoric years.

Chapter 4

New Worlds

The end of the War was the end of a chapter, and a most important chapter, in Hemingway's life. In terms of experience he had by then gone through a great many things that were to have true significance in shaping him.

He'd been exposed to the overripe softness of his mother's artistic pretensions, to the spartan way of life his father had shown him with its insistence on virile manhood. The trips into the woods of Michigan and to the Indian camps were poignant memories, filled with everlasting beauty and mystery.

He had followed in general the normal path of a well-mannered high school boy, with its conservatism, its desire for conformity, the athletics, and the pranks. He had spiced this innocent road with excursions into the streets of Chicago and Cicero, the boxing arenas. He had further rebelled, if only mildly, to breathe the heady air of freedom on these occasions when he ran away from home.

He had then come to know the real enchantment in dealing with words as a professional. The discovery that the English language could be disciplined to express exactly what he'd seen or felt had been a thrilling experience.

He had been to war. He had been severely wounded. After falling deeply in love with his nurse he had gone through the pain and the humiliation of her summary rejection.

All these things were perhaps not really unusual. They were surely not a great deal more, nor much less, than a multitude of boys of his day had gone through while growing up. Coming as they did, however, to Ernest Hemingway, they were to have lasting effect.

One thing more remained before he could call himself a writer. He needed to settle down to the bitter, grinding work in front of a typewriter. He needed to write. He needed to have behind him hundreds and thousands . . . and hundreds upon hundreds of thousands of words. He needed the humbling experience of putting them all down on paper and then throwing most of them away.

He returned home a hero. He did the usual things. Hemingway was never one to deny his public! He limped about Oak Park a bit in his uniform, using a cane. He spoke to the high school on his war experiences and displayed a pair of breeches riddled with holes—presumably the same pair of pants he'd worn in the trenches at Fossalta. He showed envious former classmates his war souvenirs. He impressed his little brother and his small fry friends as well as the citizens of Oak Park (but in entirely different ways) when he fired a souvenir star shell high over the town one night.

But the role of a hero is tiresome. Like a good many others before and after him, he discovered that the aura very quickly wears thin. As usual, his relationship with his mother was not particularly good. No doubt she felt that her son had had his fling and should begin to settle down. Nothing could have been farther from his mind. The life of a doctor, a lawyer, a businessman, least of all a concert cellist was not for him. The fling had been merely an appetizer.

Hemingway's nights were filled with insomnia and his days with frustrating idleness. He spent more and more time away from home in Cicero and Chicago. To his mother's normal catalogue of complaints she added new ones: Ernest was keeping bad company; Ernest was coming home at all hours; and many, many more.

Winter and spring dragged into summer. For a time there was the welcome relief of life up at the lake. Then that too turned sour. His mother very possibly was nagging him without mercy; and in all truth, he probably deserved it—at least some of it. He seems to have been making a mess of things. Back home the harassed Dr. Hemingway tried in the same old pattern to keep the peace between his difficult son and his wife. By the end of the summer Hemingway was apparently practically "drummed out" of the family. When everybody went back to Oak Park, there must have been universal relief when he decided to stay on at the lake by himself.

Suddenly, as though by a miracle, life changed for him. He began to work. He began to write. Week after week he kept at it. The words poured from him in a torrent. Other than school attempts and those in Italy, these were his first fiction efforts. Much of what he wrote he destroyed. Some of the stories he considered good enough to send off to magazines. They were clear, hard, incisive. They already showed in no uncertain form the diamond sharpness of scene and dialogue that was to become the Hemingway trademark.

But nobody wanted them! They were too direct. Too un-adorned. Perhaps too callous, too brutal, too close to the guts of life. The harvest of rejection slips that was to be his for a long time to come, continued.

Occasionally he took time off for lonely trips through the woods. Now and again he made a trip down to Chicago. Friends visited him: Ted Brumback, and Bill Horne, another compan-ion from the Ambulance Service in Italy. Nothing, however, interfered very long with his writing.

He stayed at the cabin through the fall and into the win-ter. He stayed until the snowflakes were falling from the skies as steadily as the rejection slips tumbled from the mailbox. Faced finally with a decision, Hemingway decided to go once again back to newspaper work. He took a job on a Canadian paper, the Toronto *Star Weekly*, the weekend edition of the Toronto *Daily Star*.

Entertainment rather than straight reporting was the re-quirement. Hemingway gave them both. He wrote feature arti-cles on everything—from a hilarious account of an adventure in a barber's college to interviews with staid politicians. He wrote on so many different subjects, with such verve and in such volume that there was real danger his growing talent would degenerate into mere fluency.

He developed an uncanny sense of audience reaction, a trait that was to become a legendary part of the Hemingway "style." He learned that actual occurrences could be reported subjectively as well as objectively without sacrificing in any way the truth. He began to trust his own reactions and to write about them in a way that was "a truer account than

[57]

anything factual can be."

One of Hemingway's maxims was "Don't do anything too bloody long." Don't wait until becoming surfeited before making a change. When the signs of boredom and restlessness begin, the time has come to move along. Accordingly, in the fall of 1920 he left the *Star Weekly* (temporarily as it turned out) and moved to Chicago for another attempt at free-lance fiction.

He stopped briefly at Oak Park. He said hello to everybody, quickly kissed the family good-bye, and was gone. But for one visit later on, this was his last trip home. He was really on his own.

Henceforward he was a writer, a professional writer. The qualifications? Simply that he *wrote*. He wrote and wrote until sometimes he fell exhausted in sleep over his typewriter.

There were other things, of course. He life was full and busy. He held the belief that a man lived but once; that life was to be enjoyed, should be lived to the limit. Nobody could or should spend every waking hour at a typewriter. He spent marvelous hours talking with friends and acquaintances. He drank and he ate in the little Italian restaurants and cafes he loved. He boxed, went to the horse races. With all his heart and spirit he enjoyed what the great city had to offer. With wide open eyes he saw and observed everything from art in the museums to the antics of broken-down boxers in the gyms.

But over everything, orchestrating his whole life was the endless clack-clack of his typewriter. When he was in places where it was impossible to use the machine, he used a pencil, leaving a trail of whittlings behind him. Wherever he went, whatever he did, words were the big things. Words and more words. Always the words down on paper that tried to express what he saw and felt, "how it was."

Until he went broke he lived in a tiny apartment on the "saloon" side of town. His neighbors were gunmen of the Prohibition era, broken-down pugs. When his money was finally gone, he moved in with his old wartime buddy, Bill Horne.

Desperate for money, he finally landed a job by answering a want ad. He was to be the editor of a trade magazine publicizing something called the Co-operative Society of America. The society was a racket run by a man named Harrison Parker. He paid Hemingway $50 a week to run the magazine and made $15,000,000 for himself from the public. Hemingway stayed with the society until "I was convinced it was crooked, stayed on a little while thinking I could write and expose it, and then decided to just rack it up as experience and the —— with it."

Once again he was broke and out of a job. This time an old Walloon Lake friend, Y. K. Smith, came to the rescue. Acquaintances of Smith who were traveling had subleased to him their huge, elegant apartment in a swanky part of town. He promptly filled the place with a conglomerate assortment of aspiring writers and painters. Hemingway was assigned sleeping space and moved in.

He soon gained the reputation of being the most colorful, the wittiest—and also the hardest working—tenant. His typewriter beat a steady tattoo, playing an industrious counterpoint to the talk and racket and general horseplay of the others. He had time for fun, he had time for observing people going about the business of living, he had time to enjoy his life. He had little time for useless talk. And his companions talked—endlessly—about Art with a capital A.

[59]

"Make a statement, Hem," somebody would say. "What do you think about Art as opposed to life?"

He snorted. "Art. Art. All that artistic stuff. The only art I'm interested in is the art of my typewriter."

As the others talked glibly about the eternal verities, and Art, mortality, and ethics, Hemingway worked. *But . . .* he also talked. *He* talked about story markets, about plot, about the problems of making words say what he wanted them to say. Art for him was the truth of life and the deathly hard business of getting it down on paper. The theme was his old one: "You can't talk about art. You've got to see it, feel it, smell it. Then write about it. If it's true, then that's art!"

He would turn, stalk upstairs, and soon the rattle of the typewriter drifted over the hum of talk of his friends. As they talked about Art, Hemingway wrestled with it, subjecting himself to the grinding, lonely discipline of trying to write about it. While others philosophized, Hem worked.

Two people passing through this bustling beehive of talk and work were to have tremendous influence on his life and his writing. One was a man, Sherwood Anderson, the brightest star of the moment in American literature. Hemingway admired Anderson and had read and re-read most of his works, particularly the famous book of short stories, *Winesburg, Ohio.* Anderson was a noted writer. Anderson was famous. Anderson was highly successful. Anderson had lived in Paris! He made an instant impression on the inhabitants of the apartment. Often he came to talk, to read them excerpts from works in progress. He was regarded as a god.

Hemingway looked and listened. Whether his respect for the great man equalled that of the others is doubtful. Writers

[*60*]

are apt to be the most egocentric people on earth. They may admire each other's work; but when writers meet, their relationship sometimes falls something short of perfection.

Anderson liked Hemingway very much and personally Hemingway liked Anderson. Often however, when the older man had left the apartment, Hemingway took great delight in criticizing vigorously Anderson's work. He considered it to be "sloppy." Justified or not, Hemingway's criticism may have really been due to the natural reaction of his own very large ego in the presence of that of the older, more polished and successful man.

Anderson was enormously fond of Hemingway and thought he had a brilliant future as a writer. There is also very little doubt that privately Hemingway was enormously impressed by Anderson's work. Hemingway's debt to Anderson in his own development as an artist is a large one. Anderson convinced Hemingway that the time was right for him to go to Europe. There were two reasons for this. One was that Hemingway needed badly the stimulus of exposure to the life and art of the Old World. The other was that living was dirt cheap in most European countries. Their currencies had been badly depressed as an aftermath of the War.

The other person who passed through this strange apartment and who became a part of Hemingway's life, was a girl, Hadley Richardson. She was attractive, sensitive, charming. She was also a very fine pianist with ambitions of her own. She was wholly in sympathy with Hemingway's hopes and dreams. They hit it off. Ernest was much impressed and so it seems was Hadley. They were married in September, 1921, at the Hemingway family cottage on the lake.

[61]

Where would they live? The atmosphere of the apartment was impossible. And also, the truth is that Hemingway had far outgrown his friends and needed a change very badly. Anderson's suggestion of Europe was enough. They would go to Paris. Ernest would write and Hadley planned to work at her music.

A trip to Toronto solved the money problem. The *Weekly Star* was glad of the prestige of having its own European correspondent, and Hemingway filled the bill exactly. The paper was to pay him on a piecework basis, including expenses. Hemingway would have to produce—or else!

Anderson gave them letters of introduction to everyone he thought they should meet in Paris. In return, just before leaving, Hemingway brought Anderson all the food remaining in their own place. Anderson wrote: "That was a nice idea, bringing thus to a fellow scribbler the food he had to abandon. . . . I remember his coming up the stairs, a magnificent, broad-shouldered man, shouting as he came."

Chapter 5

The Final Shaping

H adley and Ernest took the long, sunny route to Paris—into the Mediterranean and up through Spain. Hemingway wanted to see a bullfight. Already his absorption in this Spanish "tragedy in three acts" was beginning to claim him. He soon had his fill of the bullring, however, for the time being. Hadley was given as a trophy a rather hairless and repulsive ear of one of the bulls. The trip was a success.

These postwar years in Europe were jumbled and chaotic. The nations of the old continent were prostrate and weak and at odds with themselves from the long bloodletting. There was little stability or order anywhere.

Ernest and Hadley led lives just as rhythmless and kaleidoscopic as the world in which they lived, except for one thing: the swift forward progress Hemingway made as a man and as a writer. The years 1921 through 1924 brought him to maturity, provided the final shaping.

"What a town!" he wrote in his first letter to Sherwood Anderson about Paris. And indeed the grey old mistress of the Seine was quite a place. He and Hadley made the most of it. They wandered through the Louvre, soaking up the great art of the past. They marveled at Napoleon's tomb, stood in [...] before the statues of famous writers. They went to the [...] races, the horse races; they spent happy hours in gay outd[...] cafés. When they had money they dined like kings; when [...] were broke they lived on coffee and rolls. They listened to g[...] music, they went to plays, they organized picnics in the c[...] try. They read the classics in Sylvia Beach's Shakesp[...] Book Shop and while there rubbed shoulders with the mig[...] of the Paris' world of letters who were doing the same th[...]

As always, Hemingway kept himself in splendid phys[...] condition. He worked out long hours in gyms. He rode [...] bike. His interest in boxing continued and for a time he trai[...] and managed boxers. He became famous coaching his b[...] from their corner and reciting lines of poetry from Baudel[...] to conjure luck when the going was tough.

Hemingway entered into the sport completely. On one [...] casion one of his boxers, a young fellow named Travet, [...] taking a terrible beating from Francis Charles, a vicious fig[...] er and a potent light-heavy weight contender. Charles kno[...] Travet down and in front of several thousand roaring specta[...] began to jump on him and kick him in the groin.

Hemingway believed in boxing for keeps, but this was [...] much. It was practically legalized murder. He rushed from T[...] vet's corner, 200 pounds of outraged fury, and began to p[...] mel Charles with his fists and the water bottle. It turned in[...] "regular brannigan of a brawl" as Hemingway himself mi[...] have said, until the police rushed to Charles' rescue and pul[...] Hemingway off. He certainly saved Travet's life; but even [...] Travet never recovered from the beating.

If Paris was Ernest and Hadley's headquarters, all of [...]

rope was their playground. They returned many times to Spain for the bullfights. Hemingway was beginning to understand them and was turning into a regular *aficionado,* as a bullfight fan is called. They hiked in the Black Forest and along the Rhine in Germany. They skiied in Switzerland. They took in the sights in Italy and visited Rome. For "vacations" they journeyed to islands in the Mediterranean to enjoy the sun and swimming.

With the money exchange at 12 francs, and higher, to the dollar, it was little wonder that Paris was filling with expatriate Americans. The Left Bank of the Seine was jammed with them and many had artistic pretensions. A few, a very tiny few, were serious about their work. Hemingway had never been comfortable with poseurs and big talkers—especially about art. When they started talking about man's obligations and the duties of the artist, he began to writhe inside. True art —or whatever Hemingway would have called what he was searching for—he felt was to be found in lonely sweat at his typewriter.

His first look at the beardy pseudo-intellectuals of the Latin Quarter made him squirm. He was even more ill at ease than he had been in the apartment back in Chicago. There, he could keep by himself. In Paris, the fact that he was also an expatriate, along with the fakes, lumped him with them, he felt. He declared war. To dissociate himself from them he even went so far as to dress impeccably, amost like a dandy, as though he were the president of a big newspaper syndicate instead of a very junior grade correspondent and writer.

Sherwood Anderson had provided Hemingway with a list of serious workers whose friendship might be valuable. He lost no time in looking them up. Foremost was Gertrude Stein. She, with her companion, Alice B. Toklas, maintained a kind of salon where the working literary figures and painters used to gather for talk. Miss Stein liked Hemingway right off. He was big, he was tall; in his rather dark and handsome good looks she seemed to see real promise. Her first comment when she saw him was about his eyes. They were "interested, rather than interesting," she said.

Hemingway took his work to her. They talked, she read his writings, and she criticized them. She knew good writing from bad—she was a writer herself—and could put into words forcefully what she felt. Her criticism was hard, skillful, to the point, merciless. He recalled that she was right in everything she said. This rapport with the Misses Stein and Toklas was to continue for several years.

Other people who swarmed into Paris in the 1920's Hemingway was to know well. Most of them dropped out of sight; others became world-famous. Such people as Ezra Pound, T. S. Eliot, André Gide, and John Dos Passos were to become his lifelong friends. With them he discussed his work. From their comments he profited greatly. About one of them, Ezra Pound, be remembers that when he was right, he was very, very right, and that when he was wrong, there was no doubt about this either.

With men like these he could discuss art and what it meant to him with pleasure. He found in them responsive chords. They, like himself, were hard workers. A man might be forgiven a lot of big, high-flying talk if he also put in his long weary hours at the typewriter.

On one point Hemingway took great issue with Gertrude

Stein. She persisted in calling Hemingway and all the other young people a "lost generation." She considered them children of the war, children born of doubt. Hemingway refused to believe it. There was nothing "lost" about him. He had come to Paris to live as cheaply as he could and to learn to write as well as he could. If many of his American compatriots reveled in the term and used it as an excuse for laziness and debauchery, that was their business, not his. Furthermore, Hemingway acidly pointed out, the phrase was not even original with Miss Stein. A garage owner had used it referring to a particularly bumbling mechanic who was making a mess of repairing an automobile engine. But the name stuck. Even today it is used to describe the people of those wild 1920's.

Much criticism has been cast at Hemingway for having "copied" his way of thinking and writing from Miss Stein and others who were his friends. He is accused of being ungrateful for their having "taught" him to write. This is ridiculous and unfair, especially when directed at a man like Hemingway. Of all the authors who ever lived, he is possibly the one whose *own* style has been imitated the most.

Certainly he *learned* from other people, starting from the style sheet on the old Kansas City *Star*. That his debt is considerable cannot be denied and Hemingway himself admitted it. He learned from everyone and everything. From painters even. He said that he learned from Cézanne how to paint a scene on paper and the fact that he had never seen a bad Degas because Degas burned his bad paintings taught him to destroy his bad writing. Hemingway's critics on this score might very well recall the words of Descartes, a famous French philosopher. He said, "I see farther than those who have gone ahead of me but only because I stand on their shoulders."

Years later, Hemingway's relationship with Miss Stein cooled enormously. Her accusation that he was ungrateful is sad. The truth is that Hemingway had an enormous talent. In the early years when he was searching for ways to develop it, she was able to help. But it was *his* talent. No one else's. Of all the things that may be said about Hemingway as an artist, one thing is certain: he was brutally honest. He "stole" from no one. He worked hard to hone and sharpen his gift.

With a wife and himself to support, Hemingway had his hands full. His job as a reporter was interesting and exciting. It gave him plenty of opportunity to travel and on many of the trips Hadley was able to accompany him. There were many moments though, when the grind of journalistic writing seemed deadly. He longed to be at his own work. He had no choice, however, and so he kept at it.

Miss Stein and others of his friends continually advised him to get out of newspaper work. They felt that it was doing him more harm than good. They felt that his vital forces that should be going into creative fiction were being dissipated into the insatiable nothingness of writing news stories. Their good and well intentioned advice, however, fell with a dull thud as he felt his flat purse. And newspaper writing wasn't all bad.

Just as he had done in Toronto, he wrote on everybody and everything. His stories were a regular feature of the *Star Weekly*, and soon its companion paper, the *Star Daily* was demanding stories and assigning him specific jobs. Hemingway had learned to be an extremely skillful reporter. Furthermore, he was honest and reliable. He worked hard at gathering material. The absence of padding gave his articles a feeling of genuine quality and thoroughgoing sincerity.

In his writing, he gave the best that he had in him. Whether he was doing a down-to-earth report on a rascally cabinet minister, or a humorous account of Paris night life, it all bore the unmistakable stamp of the writer. In a sense, it was only hack work; but he brought to it the zest, the flowing drive of uncluttered words so characteristic of him when he was truly interested in a subject. And since he was a very practical young man badly in need of money, he trained himself to become interested in just about anything.

His work constantly became even more razor-edged, cleaner. Unerring accuracy in the reports was combined with drama, interest, readability. But no matter how trained or skillful or talented a man may be, good writing is no snap to produce. Hemingway stated it himself, briefly and to the point: "Easy writing makes hard reading." And vice versa. He worked like a dog.

He eventually came to write not only for his Canadian employers, but began to accept assignments from the big news services. Hearst's Universal News Service and International, and others were after his work. His fame as a newshound was growing.

While casting about in the murky political waters of postwar Europe, Hemingway managed to drag up for interviews just about every important kind of fish that swam. His sharp eye and mind drew realistic pictures of them and what they represented that were marvels of accuracy, as well as fateful prophecies for the future.

A series of ten articles on the French occupation of the Ruhr demonstrated unmistakably his personal growth as well as his increasing skill with words. He brought careful and thorough research to the work. Before he started he did his homework. As a result, he added depth and dimension far beyond anything his editor had in mind when he made the assignment. "To write about Germany," he led off, "you must begin by writing about France." He continued by digging deeply into the situation in France. "France refused in 1917 to make a peace without victory. Now she finds she has a victory without peace. To understand why this is so we must take a look at the French government." And then, with the problems of the French government disposed of, he took the next step. "What do the French people think about the Ruhr and the whole German question? You will not find out by reading the French press."

After finishing off the French background, he turned to Germany itself. In masterly scenes, written in dialogue, with dramatic climaxes just as though it were fiction, he probed the German people. On the Rhine during a riot he watched a group of furious men fighting the police. The savagery was incredible: a man grabbed an ax, slashed it into the hands of a policeman who was clinging to a bridge above the swift current. With a scream the man lost his hold and was swept into the water to death. "Why so much brutality?" Hemingway asked and then answered his own question. "Germany was never defeated in a military debacle."

His description of misery and inflation in Germany was a poignant one, chilling in its brutal description. "There are no beggars. No horrible examples on view. No visible famine sufferers nor hungry children that besiege the railway stations. The tourist leaves Germany wondering what all this starving business is about." And then the blunt truth, the evocative appraisal of Germany and the Germanic character. "For every ten professional beggars in Italy, there are a hundred amateur starvers in Germany. An amateur starver does not starve in public."

At international conferences in Genoa and Lausanne, Hemingway took his place as just one more reporter among the many who were assigned to cover the meetings. Aside from George Tchiterin, the Soviet delegate at Lausanne, who held regular press conferences, Hemingway never got near the principal figures. Reviewing the pap that was passed out in the form of official press releases, his distrust of important public figures grew. As he saw more and more of the deceit they practised and realized with what hypocrisy they betrayed the hopes of the masses of little people, he became more and more bitter about officialdom in general.

Under the tutelage of William Bolitho, the brilliant South African who represented the *Manchester Guardian,* Hemingway's nose for smelling out the untrue and the false became even more acute. He sharpened his wits to the point that it was almost instinctive for him to divine what was going on "inside," behind the facade that was presented to the public.

He came eventually to believe that in every man, power corrupts. Bolitho claimed that sooner or later one could always spot the symptoms. He even convinced Hemingway that these symptoms were evident in Hemingway's personal hero, Clemenceau, the French premier. Bolitho was very compelling. He had an exceptionally fine intellect. In addition he had a tremendous war record, which in itself was enough to cause Hemingway to listen carefully.

At this time Mussolini was the world's darling. He was the man who made the trains run on time in Italy. He was the man who was bringing order out of chaos. Hemingway did not share the general opinion of the Fascist bully. He looked over the young Fascisti battalions, the torture chambers, the murders, the blind obedience to slogans, the castor oil treatments given political enemies. Then he wrote one of the world's first completely realistic appraisals of Mussolini and Fascism. He warned against under-estimating him. "[He] isn't a fool, and he is a great organizer."

Hemingway varied his attacks in as many ways as he knew how. "Get hold of a good photograph of Signor Mussolini sometime and study it. You will see the weakness in his mouth which forces him to scowl the famous Mussolini scowl that is imitated by every 19 year old Fascisto in Italy. Study his past record. . . . Study his genius for clothing small ideas in big words. . . ."

Hemingway defined the Fascist psychology. "[They] make no distinction between socialists, communists, republicans or members of co-operative societies. They are all Reds and dangerous." These were powerful and perceptive words and opinions for a 23 year old from Oak Park, Illinois, attempting to get at the essence of a political morality. They were far beyond their time and they are still words to ponder in the confused world of today.

Hemingway's description of Fascism was mocking and alert. His was among the first voices raised in strong protest at what was to become the agony of the times. Years later, stung when accused of literary irresponsibility, Hemingway cried out at his critics: "Having fought Fascism in every place I know how, in the places where you really fight it, I have no remorse —neither literary nor political."

In 1922 the Turkish liberator Kemal Pasha drove the Greeks out of Asia Minor. Hemingway was sent to cover the exodus. Some of his writing in this period is indeed some of the finest newspaper reporting ever done. His primary concern was with troops and campaigns, but the spectacle of the Greek refugees pouring wearily, 250,000 of them, across the torn earth toward Greece stirred him as few other things had done. Always quick and generous in his response to human grief, Hemingway was scarred beyond belief by this refugee misery. He had never seen nor imagined such suffering as he saw along the road to Adrianople that October of 1922.

His experience gave new dimenison to his status as a fine reporter, as a man, and as a writer. He painted quick scenes with strokes of sure mastery, much as Goya might have done on canvas. Against a blurred, drear background small clear pinpoints shone in heartbreaking relief. As, for example, "In a never-ending, staggering march the Christian population of Eastern Thrace is jamming the roads toward Macedonia. The main column crossing the Maritza river at Adrianople is twenty miles long. Twenty miles of carts drawn by cows, bullocks and muddy-flanked water buffalo, with exhausted, staggering men, women and children, blankets over their heads, walking blindly in the rain beside their worldy goods."

Thirty years later Hemingway recalled that he was so shaken by what he had seen it was difficult to stick to his career. "I remember," he said, "coming home from the Near East . . . absolutely heartbroken at what was going on and in Paris trying to decide whether I would put my whole life into trying to

[73]

do something about it or to be a writer." This from the man who is said by some to be the apostle of violence and brutality! He continued, "I decided, cold as a snake, to be a writer and to write as truly as I could all my life."

And what of this writer?

As Hemingway played, boxed, skiied, and hiked over Europe, and as he earned his keep as a practising newspaperman, what was happening to the *real* writer? The one we are most interested in. He worked. Night and day, between and during assignments, in every free moment he had.

He wrote a little poem which was published in 1923. It was a kind of little ode in which he referred to his typewriter as a *mitrailleuse*, the French word for machine gun.

> *The mills of the gods grind slowly,*
> *But this mill*
> *Chatters in mechanical staccato.*
> *Ugly short infantry of the mind,*
> *Advancing over difficult terrain*
> *Make this Corona*
> *Their mitrailleuse.*

Hemingway's Corona never stopped chattering as he fought his lonely battle. The loneliness of this battle is one of the things that makes it so difficult to write dramatically about writers. Outwardly they may do things which are tremendously exciting—or extremely dull—but that exterior is only the shadow of the struggle going on quietly inside. The private battle, which can only be guessed at, is the most exciting.

Life, people, and the things they do are sometimes awfully complicated. Since people are a writer's raw material, he must then write about complicated happenings. But his thinking must not be confused or his writing will be confused and this is sure death! He must write simply and clearly about complicated matters. To do so, he must understand them, not merely judge. Hemingway himself said the same thing: "As a writer you should not judge. You should understand."

Most people judge without understanding. The writer's task is just the opposite. Most people are never called upon to expose the state of their inner selves. Again, a writer's position is just the reverse. If what a writer writes is to be good, and true—and it must be if it is going to endure—he must understand, and to understand, he must purify himself and his thinking. He must accomplish this in the face of his own humanness, for writers are not "different" from anyone else. They don't like to do difficult, unnatural things any more than the next man.

It is a battle of the heart, and this battlefield is a lonely one, and very apt to be a bloody one. It leaves marks and scars on the man. Sometimes these scars are apt to make writers difficult to live with. Hemingway developed abrasive qualities that cost him dearly; sometimes the price was almost unbearable. He could take criticism but not contradiction. Basically the kindest and most generous of men, he nonetheless made enemies and estranged friends who should have remained dear to him.

The extent of the inner battles of Ernest Hemingway can never be known. The battles can be understood only through the characters he wrote about, and through his public life. In some ways, however, Hemingway is less difficult to understand than other writers, since he tended to write as he lived and to live as he wrote.

Meantime, in Paris in the early 1920's, he fought his battles, those on the inside and the apparent ones on the outside. He was stubborn about his work; along about now it began to pay off, even if only very slightly.

In January of 1923, six of his poems were published in *Poetry 21,* a little magazine published in Paris. A bit later, in the *Little Review,* another small magazine, six of his stories appeared. In the summer of 1923, Robert McAlmon, a "nine-hundred horse-power linotype publisher" brought out a book that was all Hemingway's, *Three Stories and Ten Poems.* Nothing very great, but still it was a book of his own.

One of these stories, "My Old Man" is considered by many to be among the best short stories of that year. Edward O'Brien later included it in his volume *The Best Short Stories of 1923.* The name of the author was misspelled—*Hemenway* he was called. And this was all. Nothing more published. Though he continued to bombard the publishers of magazines at home with his work (these people paid in real money, not just with prestige!), nobody was interested. The editors said that his works were not stories at all. They called them merely sketches, or vignettes, to Hemingway's despair—and fury.

During this period, disaster struck once, hard. While Hemingway was covering the conference in Lausanne, his wife Hadley came to join him from Paris. She brought with her, carefully typed and catalogued, all the work he had done thus far—many, many stories, poems, and a large piece of a novel. The briefcase containing the work was stolen from her compartment. There were no copies! Hemingway was nearly out of his mind. Except for a few stories in the mails, the work of years was gone. He said he would rather have submitted to surgery than to have endured this loss. Bitterly, and sadly, he started all over again, nearly from scratch.

More and more he was devoting time to fiction at the expense of the revenue-producing newspaper work. Money became really tight and then one bright morning Hadley gave him a bit of news. She was going to have a child!

Gertrude Stein recalls that he came to her apartment in the morning, stayed silently through lunch, tea, and dinner. He finally announced, dolefully, "I am too young to be a father." She and Miss Toklas consoled him as best they could. "It will all work out somehow," they insisted. Characteristically, Hemingway did not wait for things to work out before making a decision. He decided they would return to Toronto for two years, where he had been offered a reporter's job at $125 a week, a princely salary in those days, and not bad for a reporter even now.

This was an honorable solution to the crisis, but it must have called for all of Hemingway's fortitude. He was fed up to the teeth with newspaper work; he was working well now at his fiction and plans for more stories and a full scale novel were forming in his mind. He was arriving at an important period of transition in his work and the news of this expected child upset them all. In August, 1923, he and Hadley sailed for Toronto, where their son was born.

At first things went very well. Too well. Hemingway was the boy wonder, the fellow who had written all those famous dispatches from Europe. They had in their own way contributed toward making the Toronto *Star* one of Canada's giants in the newspaper field.

Differences soon arose, however, between Hemingway and Harry Comfort Hindmarsh, assistant managing editor of the paper. Hemingway nearly exploded when he was assigned to do nature studies in the park. This assignment was too much for the young man who had so recently done cogent and penetrating studies of such people as Clemenceau and Mussolini. The final break came when Hemingway interviewed Count Aponyi, the famed Hungarian diplomat. Aponyi lent Hemingway certain official documents with the understanding that they were to be returned as soon as the paper was through with them. This information was duly passed on to Hindmarsh, but somehow the documents wound up in his wastebasket and were subsequently burned.

Hemingway promptly quit his job. By January of 1924, scarcely four months after they had departed, the Hemingway family—three of them now—was back in Paris.

He was free at last from the burden of having to jump when the editor of a newspaper spoke. He was possessed of an overmastering drive to settle down and write fiction. He was also nearly flat broke, with a wife and infant son dependent upon him.

Chapter 6

The Sun Rises

When Ernest and Hadley and little John Hadley Nicanor Hemingway (Nicanor after a much admired bullfighter, Nicanor Villalta) returned to Paris, they faced immediately a full share of the very real problems.

They were broke, or nearly so. Hemingway had no job. His row with Harry Comfort Hindmarsh had effectively cut him off from the Toronto *Star*. Far more to the point, though, than this simple loss of employment was the fact that Hemingway had reached a point where he probably wouldn't have taken a newspaper job even if one had been available.

His notes, his journals and his head as well, were filled with plans for essays, poems, stories. Most pressing of all were the novels he felt he had to write. These were not short works that could be done quickly. On the contrary, they were full-scale, long-range projects needing months and even years of concentrated effort. He was on fire with the necessity of getting them down. Every fiber of his being as a writer, an artist, cried out to him not to delay. The emotional demand to be at this highly creative work drove all consideration of a newspaper job from his mind.

Balanced against this overpowering need was the simple problem of money. Money meant warmth, food, clothing; and these things too had an urgency all their own. Hadley looked glumly about the tiny flat.

"Screeeeeech. . . . Screeeeeech!" The whining scream of the power saw in the mill below their flat set her teeth on edge. She looked at her husband. He was lying on a mattress on the floor, their bed, covered with blankets. About him was a litter of paper and pencil shavings. He scribbled industriously.

Nothing distracted Hemingway from his writing.

She looked at her son. Bumby, for so he had been nicknamed, was sleeping peacefully in his carriage. It was huge, the last word in elegant conveyances for babies. That darn carriage, she thought, the most elegant baby carriage in all of Paris— and we don't even have enough to eat. Or enough fuel for that joke of a stove.

"Screeeeeech. . . . ." whined the saw. Ernest wrote on.

Bumby stirred, smiled in his sleep. He was utterly peaceful.

Hadley shivered against the cold, wandered over to the window. Outside, a gigantic chestnut tree raised its bare branches to the sky. The street was filled with sludgy snow, melting and dirty. At least, at least, she thought, winter will soon be over, and in the spring and summer we'll be able to stay warm.

There was a footstep outside. She whirled. She looked at Ernest. He jumped out of the bed, strode to the door. At least this was a sound to which he was in tune. A sheaf of letters tumbled through the slot. Impatiently he tore them open, one by one. With each letter, with each rejection slip, his face grew tighter, grimmer. "Sketches . . . vignettes . . . not even stories," he said. "They don't know what writing is. They wouldn't recognize a story if Tolstoy himself sent them one."

He opened the last envelope, glanced at it, threw it on the floor. He returned to the mattress, covered himself up, and the eternal scribbling began again.

Idly Hadley glanced through the mail. The same thing. Over and over again. Would it never end? She looked at the last letter. Suddenly her face changed, darkened. She read it through again, carefully. Then she walked over to the mattress.

"Ernest," she said, waving the letter. "Did you read this one?"

He glanced up. "Yes . . . sure I read it. What about it?"

She was incredulous. "What *about* it? What do you mean?"

"I mean it means nothing to me."

"Nothing to you?" She could scarcely believe her ears. The letter was an offer from a Hearst syndicate of a permanent job as European correspondent at a salary that was high enough to keep them practically in luxury as long as they wished.

"No. That's right. They know what they can do with their job. I don't want it. I've told you I'm through writing that crud for the newspapers."

"But Ernest," she pleaded, "can't you do like you did before? Write what you want on the side? It wouldn't take too much of your time to do a few articles for the paper."

"I'm through I tell you. I'm through. However little time it takes—it's too much. Don't ask me again."

Hadley stiffened. "All right, Mr. Tolstoy," she said, "Write what you want. But let me tell you right now there's nothing in the house to eat. What are your plans for that?"

Hemingway grunted. He put away the papers and the stub of a pencil, walked to a wardrobe and got out his clothes.

"The taxi?" she said sarcastically. "Or is it vegetables today?"

Hemingway threw his wife an angry glance and stomped out the door. She went to the window and watched him stride along the street below. Wearily she leaned her head against the pane. That awful taxi she thought. How she hated it. Why was her husband so stubborn? Hurtling about Paris driving that squawking taxi to pick up a few francs. Or unloading vegetables in the markets from the trucks for a few centimes or a handful of carrots. To do things like these and then turn down such a marvelous chance with a newspaper syndicate. She sighed, trying to understand. Basically Hadley was a gentle woman. She couldn't stay angry long. She turned to the Bumby who was stirring in the ridiculous, gigantic baby carriage.

Hemingway strode across the park. He paused a moment

[82]

in front of a bust of the French writer Flaubert. Flaubert looked cold. Hemingway *was* cold. The holes in his beret and in the ragged grey turtleneck sweater he was wearing allowed free passage to the icy winter air.

Hours later Hadley heard her husband's step as he bounded up the stairs. He burst in the door, his eyes glowing. "We eat," he cried, putting down packages. "And we're going to be warm, too." He stoked the stove with shavings and coal. Soon it was blazing merrily.

Hadley started to prepare supper on the little table. Wearily she looked at what he had brought. "I don't mind for myself, Ernest," she said, "I'm used to it. But is Bumby supposed to eat rolls and fried potatoes too? All the time?"

"No sir. Not Bumby. Nothing too good for him. Look in the other bag." Fatuously Hemingway turned to the little boy and started to play with him. Hadley shook her head, started serving. She stared at her husband. "Ernest," she said, grimly, "This can't go on. Something's going to give."

"What do you mean it 'can't go on'?" His face darkened with mounting anger. "It's going to go on. It *is* going on. If you don't like it you know what you can do."

"All right. So I know what I can do. Well, one of these days . . ." She stopped. There was no use quarreling. Tempers were already too short and the fights between them daily grew more bitter.

Hemingway stared at her, his face hard and uncompromising. Then he relaxed, turned back to the child.

He picked up Bumby, stood him on the floor in front of the chair. "Now, Bumby," he said, "I want you to learn this. In case you ever get lost, all you have to do is say it and some nice person will bring you home."

Over and over he repeated the bit of doggerel and after him the childish voice repeated the words.

> *"Dix bis avenue des Gobelins*
> (Ten and one-half Gobelins Avenue)
> *Dix bis avenue des Gobelins,*
> *Dix bis avenue des Gobelins,*
> That's where my Bumby lives!

These lines became famous many, many years later.

And so Hemingway worked. He worked his heart out. But it was never enough. As the months passed, as the seasons rolled around, the rejection slips tumbled through the slot in the door.

Nobody wanted his work enough to pay for it.

He wrote and he wrote and he wrote. When the typewriter ribbons were beaten to shreds he retreated to the cheaper, and just as reliable, pencil stubs. When the whine of the saw in the mill below was too screeching, or when Bumby cried too loud, or when it was too cold even for him in the flat, he retired to some nearby café. In a back corner he worked until his eyes bugged from weariness.

The arguments in the Hemingway household must have been classic. The complaints on each side were honest ones. They were both hotheaded. Bullheadedly he stuck to his course even though in time he must have known in his heart that the constant erosion of such a life made the situation hopeless.

It wasn't all bad of course. In these days Hemingway was still on good terms with the Stein-Toklas salon. These two ladies did what they could to make things easier. They fussed about young Bumby and became sponsors when he was baptized. They embroidered and knitted warm little clothes for him and no doubt had the hungry Hemingways to an occasional meal.

Nobody, even if they're threadbare and half hungry, can live the life of a hermit. There were happy times as before. Outings in the woods and parks in good weather, the bike races, the fights, and talk in the cafés helped to relieve the monotonous grind. Paris was too big and too vital. It was impossible for anyone to be buried in it all alone. Its life swirled enticingly through the streets and boulevards and the cafés.

Hemingway's reputation in his own country was less than nothing. In Paris, though, he was beginning to be recognized as a possible comer. As he passed along the sidewalks, threading his way through the tables, there were smiles of welcome and invitations to join various groups. The opinions and thoughts of the handsome, big American were coming to be respected. He was known as a man who could not be bought. He would knuckle under to no one. His ideals were impregnable. His devotion to his work, and his capacity to produce it, were awesome.

So, on one side of the balance, this was a time of grinding work, despair, and bleakness. On the other, the creative side, it was a time of rare joy and happiness.

In 1924, the *transatlantic review* was started by the famous English writer, Ford Madox Ford. Hemingway and Ford became firm and admiring friends. Ultimately Hemingway was to function as part-time editor and talent scout for the magazine. The *transatlantic* became the best known of all the little magazines. It served the double purpose of offering fine criticism to aspiring writers and as a place where newcomers

[*85*]

could be printed.

In his capacity as scout for the *transatlantic,* Hemingway was able to get Gertrude Stein's *The Making of Americans* published serially. He assisted her in a final desperate burst to make a deadline by dusting off the manuscript from the shelf where it had lain and typing up the first badly needed 50 pages.

Meantime, things were looking up for Hemingway, in a modest sort of way. Another book of his was about ready to come off the press.

in our time was a handsome little book—if a booklet of 32 pages can really be called a book! It was printed on a hand press on beautiful paper and was a real little gem of the printer's craft. One hundred and seventy copies were made. In later years, each one of them was to become a collector's item.

Hemingway saw to it that he got a good press in the *transatlantic review*! In all fairness the book deserved a good press. The review reads like a preview of all the reviews of Hemingway's work he was to produce in later years.

The reviewer commented that the work pinpointed those "moments when life is condensed and clean-cut and significant, presenting them in minute narratives that eliminate every useless word. Each tale is much longer than the measure of its lines."

Throughout his whole career Hemingway was known to inject an enormous part of himself into his characters. In *in our time* appeared Nick Adams, his first fictional hero. Nick moves through the stories in a background so identical to Hemingway's own that identification is unavoidable.

In these stories published in *in our time* and in subsequent Nick Adams stories, appear for the first time the full stylistic magic of Hemingway's prose, the spare, lean style. He writes about things *as they were,* as he truly observed them, not simply as he *thought* they were.

Consider, for example, how Nick sees the trout in a pool in "Big Two-Hearted River." "He watched them holding themselves with their noses in the current, many trout in deep, fast moving water, slightly distorted as he watched far down through the glassy convex surface of the pool, its surface pushing and swelling smooth against the resistance of the log-driven piles of the bridge. At the bottom of the pool were the big trout. Nick did not see them at first. Then he saw them at the bottom of the pool, big trout looking to hold themselves on the gravel bottom in a varying mist of gravel and sand, raised in spurts by the current."

About this time Scott Fitzgerald was one of the brightest stars of American writing. Scott showed up in France partly to taste the gay night life of Paris and to mingle in the doings of the rich international set, and partly to sample the atmosphere, the talk, and the company of the serious artists. Inevitably Hemingway and Fitzgerald met.

Two men more dissimilar on the surface could hardly have been found. Hemingway despised the rich idlers and sophisticated triflers that Fitzgerald seemed to adore. In spite of this they hit it off immediately. Each was perceptive enough to separate the outer "public" man from the inner writing man. They found in each other qualities of complete dedication and absolute, uncompromising integrity. Scott was certain that Hemingway would become one of the great writers of all time.

Now started one of those incomprehensible chains of in-

Hemingway and Fitzgerald were both eager students of writing.

terlocking events that had direct bearing on all of Hemingway's future relationships with the publishing world in the United States. Hemingway's old friend, Sherwood Anderson was tremendously impressed with *in our time.* He interceded with his own publishers, Boni & Liveright, on behalf of Hemingway, to bring out an American edition. Scott Fitzgerald read the book and was also impressed. Immediately he started writing letters to get the book published in the United States by *his* publisher, Scribner's. Anderson was riding high at Boni & Liveright; Fitzgerald was the fair-haired boy at Scribner's.

It must have been a big moment in the icy little flat over the sawmill. Not one, but *two,* big publishers were making bids. Boni & Liveright cabled; Scribner's wrote. The letter of the Scribner's editor, Maxwell Perkins, was a long time coming because it had an insufficient address. Dwellers in garrets are apt to have trouble getting mail regularly. Furthermore, Boni & Liveright offered an immediate advance of $200—all the money in the world at this time to the battered and tattered Hemingways. Hemingway accepted by return cable.

Very likely he would have preferred to have gone with Scribner's if for no other reason than that association with the famed Maxwell Perkins would have been to his liking. Meanwhile though, there was that signed contract on the rickety table and at the moment nothing else mattered.

Contracts make heavy reading, but in this one there was a loophole. It was to do much to influence Hemingway's career as a writer and to provide gossipy tongues with an enormous amount of speculation about him as a man. The contract stated that if Boni & Liveright did not accept his second book within 60 days, they forfeited their right to it—and to the third.

In Our Time came out in the United States, this time in capital letters, in October, 1925. It was more like a real book now. It had been enlarged with more stories and was 214 pages. Nick Adams revealed more and more of his past, and in doing so, gave a broader look at Hemingway's own life. The price was even big—$2. They printed 1,335 copies. The best that can be said is that Hemingway had his advance! If publishers were interested in his work now, readers still weren't. Several other publishers picked up their ears when they glanced through the book, took in its concise, spare style, the crystal-like clarity. Then they relaxed. The brief flurry was over.

Hemingway, however, had the $200 in his pocket and a novel in his head. What more could a writer ask? The book he planned was to be a tragedy, with the forever abiding earth as its hero. The location was to be Europe and the people would be lost people—tragic products of the war. The story would come out of his own experience and out of the quest for the essence of that experience.

"There is only one thing to do with a novel," Hemingway told Scott Fitzgerald, "and that is to go straight on through to the end of the———thing." So spoke Hemingway, who had never written a novel.

If he knew how to write it, he also knew where to write it "Pack up," he said to Hadley. "We're going to Spain." Except for his homeland, Spain was for Hemingway the land he loved the best, and the place he worked the best.

She sniffed a bit sarcastically. "So we're going to Spain. Just like that. And live on $200 while you write a novel?"

"Just like that," he said emphatically. "We'll manage somehow. We're going to Spain."

A bit suspiciously—she was suspicious of nearly everything these days—the gentle but stubborn Hadley got her things together and they were on their way.

It was a whirlwind trip. In Valencia, on July 21, 1925, his 26th birthdate, Hemingway started the novel. They never stopped moving. Apparently following the bullfight circuit they took in Madrid, San Sebastian, and Hendaye, as well as intermediate points. They were back in Paris by September 6th. They returned with a lot of fine memories and—nobody will ever know how he did it—the manuscript of a completed novel.

This first draft of Hemingway's first novel was written in exactly forty-eight writing days. He practically knocked himself out in the process. He seemed to have been following his own advice to Fitzgerald. He was to regret it later when the time came to rewrite. Considerably chastened, he later said about the book: "I knew nothing about writing a novel when I started it and so wrote too fast and each day to the point of complete exhaustion. So the first draft was very bad. . . . I had to rewrite it completely. But in the rewriting I learned much."

Once back in Paris he set the draft aside for a time to give it a chance to jell and to give his own mind a chance to refresh itself. Life continued about as before. Old friendships moved along and newer ones blossomed, particularly that with Scott Fitzgerald. The common bond between them strengthened. They were both real writing men, honest, sincere, and hardworking. Each of them, all his life long, was to remain the avid student of the art of words, the way to put them together to make them say what you want to say.

Between drafts of the big novel, Hemingway devoted himself to another project. In seven days he produced a book he called *The Torrents of Spring*. The fight it touched off rages to this day.

Boni & Liveright were committed to take his next book. If they turned it down within 60 days, they also forfeited the third book and he would be free of his contract with them. They turned down *The Torrents of Spring* flatly. In no uncertain terms they refused to have anything to do with it, and thereby they made a mistake they must have regretted for all time.

Hemingway could now go where he chose—to Scribner's and Maxwell Perkins along with Scott Fitzgerald.

Scribner's must have grinned slyly when they first saw *The Torrents of Spring*. It was no sooner out than the controversy exploded. The reason for Boni & Liveright's rejection became clear. In sly, sardonic language, and in the very acid style of which Hemingway was already a master, he poked fun at the way that Gertrude Stein and, what was even worse—at the way Boni & Liveright's prize author, Sherwood Anderson, wrote.

Anderson was forgiving, even though completely undeserving of such an attack. He was a real professional writer, and in spite of the fact that the book made his own writing appear foolish, he was big enough to appreciate the sure mastery of Hemingway's writing. Gertrude Stein could not overlook the book. Relations between her and Hemingway had already been severely strained. This book was the limit! Perhaps not an implacable foe, she became certainly for the rest of her life a bitter commentator on Ernest Hemingway and his work.

The real reasons Hemingway wrote *The Torrents of Spring* will probably never be known. Some said he cold-bloodedly wrote a book pillorying Anderson in such a way that Boni & Liveright could not possibly publish it, thus freeing Hemingway from his contract with them. Others said he set out to try to destroy both Anderson and Stein in a spirit of real professional jealousy and malice. Still others claimed he was sick and tired of hearing that he had been taught to write by them, that he didn't have any real talent of his own, and wanted to get it off his chest. At any rate, from Hemingway's point of view he was justified or he wouldn't have written the book.

From theirs—particularly Gertrude Stein's—it was unjustified. There the matter rests.

Hemingway settled down now and devoted himself to the task of revising "the" book. The total writing time for the first novel, including the 48 day first draft, was a full nine months. He wrote his heart out and the results justified it. Some people claimed that Hemingway was a good story writer, but was "only" a short story writer. They said he didn't have the depth or the ability to endure the long, sustained effort necessary to produce a major novel.

When *The Sun Also Rises* was published in October, 1926, there was no longer any doubt. It was a remarkable book. Its admirers claimed it to be one of the great books of the century. If not quite this, it certainly was one of the finest that had been written for a long, long time. Drawing deeply from the meanings in his own life. Hemingway created a work that was not only exciting as a story but also summed up in part the moral dilemma of the first part of this century.

There is really only *one* story, they say, for men to tell each other: the classic story of the struggle between good and evil. Hemingway tried to tell this story. He wrestled with its deepest implications and meanings.

The novel is set in Spain. As its people move across the pages in a torrent of clear, spare, and highly evocative prose, the reader becomes aware that he is involved in this classic struggle. What is beautiful and good is in bright contrast to what is ugly and vile. Eternal values are set in conflict with transitory ones—the vanities, the fragile frailities of human nature, all that is likely to be rampant in a postwar period.

On the inscription page of *The Sun Also Rises* Hemingway attempted to quash once and for all that hated phrase of Gertrude Stein's regarding the "lost generation." He quoted first from her: "You are all a lost generation". And then to destroy the label forever (and also to provide him his title), he quoted from the Bible, the book of Ecclesiastes: "One generation passeth away, and another generation cometh: but the earth abideth forever. . . . The sun also ariseth, and the sun goeth down, and hasteth to his place where he arose. . . . The wind goeth toward the south, and turneth about unto the north; it whirleth about continually, and the wind returneth again according to his circuits. . . . All the rivers run into the sea; yet the sea is not full; unto the place from whence the rivers come, thither they return again."

Alas! This did not kill the label. In trying to prove Gertrude Stein wrong, Hemingway was generally misunderstood. Possibly the world didn't have time to digest the magnificent words from the Bible. At any rate, the label stuck and what was worse, he was proclaimed the prophet of the lost generation!

To his dying day Hemingway denied the accusation and tried to correct the misunderstanding, but it was useless. Stein's phrase stuck in people's minds.

The Sun Also Rises made Ernest Hemingway famous. From then on he was his own man, to write and live as he pleased—as much as it is given to any one to write or to live as he pleases.

But there was one saddening aspect to his triumph. Ernest Hemingway and Hadley parted. She was a woman, with all a woman's instincts and needs for care, a home, and security. Ernest was a man and an honorable one. He was aware of

Hadley's feelings. But he was also a writer, and a fine one.

Much insight into Hemingway comes from the characters in his books and stories. One of them says, and if it is not all Hemingway, it is certainly partly him: "What I had to do was work. I did not care, particularly, how it all came out. . . . They all wanted something that I did not want and I would get it without wanting it, if I worked. To work was the only thing, it was the only thing that always made you feel good, and in the meantime it was my own————life and I would lead it where and how I pleased."

Hemingway was deeply tormented by the situation. There is no doubt about it. It was made additionally painful because he had fallen in love with someone else—Pauline Pfeiffer, an American girl who worked in the Paris office of the fashion magazine *Vogue*. Pauline was chic, quick on the uptake, and much fun. She, Hadley and Ernest spent a great deal of time together, and somehow, it happened.

By nature, Hemingway was a tremendously loyal person. He was tortured, and torn almost to the point of collapse. "There is no suffering," he said, "like that of a man in love with two women at the same time."

The emotional structure of Hadley's and Ernest's relationship had been destroyed. The success, the money, the fame had come too late to be of any help. The marriage was finished.

Hadley was a dreamy, impractical girl. She was also very lovely and sweet. When matters came to a head she bowed out most gracefully, and, perhaps, with some relief. She was probably very tired and weary of it all. There was little bitterness. Hadley divorced Ernest, packed up her things, and with Bumby returned to America.

The Sun Also Rises was dedicated to Hadley. As if to put a final honorable seal on the past, Hemingway assigned the royalties of the book to her and his son. He bought some new and fine clothes. He had his hair cut regularly now by a barber. His moustache was trimmed to a handsome and formidable black brush. He drank good cognac instead of cheap wine. Once again he was the handsome and dapper man about town and the fun spots of Europe.

People listened to what he said. They watched what he did and repeated it later with embellishments of their own. They imitated his styles of clothing, his taste in food and liquor. Ernest Hemingway became the rage and he enjoyed it to the hilt. His blustering ego lapped up his new fame.

His faith in himself, his unshakable faith in the magic of the words he knew so well how to manage was justified.

The sun had risen.

The legend of the public Hemingway also began to take final shape. The public was not disappointed.

Chapter 7

The Legend

H ow does a legend grow?

As the years passed, how did Hemingway's grow? How did his public image sustain itself? What nourished it? We start with a little kernel of fact. For example: remember that once in Paris Hemingway jumped into a ring and physically stopped a fighter named Charles from beating a groggy opponent to death. The battle between Hemingway and Charles was broken up by the police.

What followed? As time went by, in gyms, cafés, and clubs all over France and the United States, good fellows got together to talk: "Did you hear how old Hem knocked out the middleweight champion of France?"

"Yeah, yeah. I heard something about it. What really happened?"

"I was there, so I know."

And then the goggle-eyed listener heard what "really happened." Each time the story was told, the version was different, bloodier—and Hemingway's prowess and quickness with his fists grew.

Hemingway didn't bother to deny or confirm the stories.

He was a very busy man, dedicated to his writing and to enjoying life. He'd also learned from his efforts to quash the "lost generation" label just how futile it could be to try to set the record straight. Furthermore, if the truth were known, the stories probably tickled him.

Nevertheless, he was a man of scrupulous honesty. Later, when asked directly about the fight, he had this to say: "Any sane person knows that writers do not knock out middleweight champions—unless the writer's name happens to be Gene Tunney!"

So the story grew. The facts that Hemingway was an excellent boxer, loved the sport, and spent long hours in the ring sparring, seemed to confirm it.

Many people think that this episode with Charles was really the start of "the" Hemingway legend. With the passage of time and as he moved about the earth to far and sometimes dangerous places, everything that he did, or that happened to him grew all out of proportion. It was magnified and distorted to one end: to prove he was the biggest, roughest, toughest apostle of violence and blood that ever walked.

The stories were endless; they took in every aspect of his life. His was the wildest boyhood that any youngster ever had. No one had performed such feats of heroism as he performed in the trenches at Fossalta. He seldom took a bite of solid food—preferring the quicker action of cognac, rum, or absinthe. No woman was safe within a mile of him. He swaggered, he snarled, he roared and raged. He stared down charging rhinos and finally dropped them within inches of his rifle with one shot between the eyes. He caught the biggest marlin and tuna that ever swam, and when they weren't biting he went after them with a Thompson submachine gun. He had a standing offer for years of $200 to anyone who could stay four rounds in a ring with him. The finest Spanish *matador* was a piker whenever Big Ernie took it into his head to get in a bullfight. Struggling young writers didn't dare get within a mile of him or he'd tear their heads off.

And so on and on and on. . . .

What really happened? Basically Hemingway was an enormously gentle and honest man. He once told a friend: "Sometimes it is necessary to write a bitter letter, a hurtful letter. When I have to do this I always file it away for a week in a drawer to give myself a chance to cool off." How did a man like this come to project such a public image of himself? There are a number of reasons; and if they are understood, then a much clearer picture of Hemingway emerges.

First of all, as in the case of the boxer Francis Charles, in nearly all the stories, there is a fantastic nubbin of truth. Hemingway loved the talk and excitement and companionship of men in cafés and cantinas. He was vital, highly aware always of what was going on around him. He loved the heightening of his senses that he got from alcohol. So he drank his share of what was available. Possibly more than his share. But he was far from being a dissolute alcoholic. The quantity and the discipline and the clarity of his work did not come from a befuddled mind.

Hemingway was a man—a powerful, virile human being. He loved women. He tended perhaps to over-romanticize them, put them on pedestals. Perhaps this is one of the reasons so many of his marriages ended disastrously. He was divorced three times and married four times in his life. Each of his wives he loved deeply and the breakups hurt him. But he was far from being a rake to frighten decent women.

He had a temper—there's no doubt about this. But he also made real efforts to control it. Because of his reputation he was constantly provoked. "So you're the big shot Ernest Hemingway," a drunk might say. "Well, I don't think you're that tough." Thereupon the man would take a swing at him and he'd have to do something about it. Another juicy bit would be added to the legend.

Hemingway was also a very forthright man, which is far different from being bad-tempered. Sometimes though, the effect is the same. When deeply offended, or when confronted by something he knew not to be the truth, he sounded off in no uncertain terms, but only after vigorous reflection.

Like his father, he was a fine shot with either a rifle or a shotgun. He loved to hunt, to enjoy the outdoors—and he did so all his life. This is no reason, however, to make him a ruthless killer who stalked the earth from one end to the other with blazing guns. Or to see him as a man who, out of sheer savagery and delight in danger, ran tremendous risks with great beasts. A first rate hunter usually acts just the opposite.

He was also a fine fisherman. In later years, when he lived in Key West and in Cuba, the lure of the deep, blue, swirling Gulf Stream claimed him almost daily. He loved to go after the gigantic fish that swam in these waters and some of his catches were record ones. Hemingway was always an early riser, preferring to work from the darkness of the predawn hours until midday. In the afternoons, fishing the Gulf was his relaxation, his way of unwinding the knots after the concentrated hours at the typewriter. On these fishing trips arms were always carried on board. There are huge and fearsome creatures in these seas. Sometimes, it is true, a submachine gun was taken and was used with deadly precision on enormous sharks.

At one time in Key West he built a small boxing ring up at one end of the town. The "famous" $200 was prize money he put up as he tried to promote and train clever young local boys as professionals.

Bullfighting was also dear to Hemingway. He studied it and very possibly knew more about it than any other American who ever lived. His respect for the *toreros* was enormous. He knew well that the end of the "game" was intended to be death. He made a few early and preliminary tries in the bull-ring himself, but soon gave it up. A quick and painful death in this manner was not for him. He picked himself up from the sand, dusted his breeches, and went back to his seat and his typewriter. "That————bull was made of cement," he said ruefully.

His hatred for young and struggling writers was supposed to be notorious. He was jealous of competition, fearful for his position, so people said. He wouldn't lift a finger to help anybody, one of the most unfair of all accusations. He was unbelievably generous with his time in such ways. He was quick and generous with praise and just as quick and to the point with something he didn't like.

He'd look up from a manuscript he liked, grin, perhaps feint and shadowbox in that manner of his. "Look, kid, it's good, good. Keep at it." On a manuscript that was good, but that also was written in obvious imitation of his own style, he'd say, "Look kid, it's good, but don't try to write like I do. There's no future in it."

For something he didn't like, his comments were apt to be bellowed, angrily. Of all things, Hemingway loved words and hated sloppy, self-indulgent writers. Devastatingly, and with sarcasm that bit deep, he'd roar, "Why don't you write all in clichés? It's a lot easier."

So the legend of the bull of American letters stemmed partly from the kind of life he led. In all the stories about him there was the germ of truth. He was always somewhere something was happening! Furthermore, Hemingway himself was a professional storyteller. He loved a good story, and no doubt in his own talk there was a great deal that enhanced his growing reputation as a fabulous character.

Wherever he went he found a public ready either to offer adulation or insults. From the Stork and Twenty-One Clubs in New York to the El Caribe in Key West, to a multitude of bars in Havana, he enjoyed life, and the legend grew. His personality was magnetic, compelling, his generosity and hospitality famous. People of all kinds gravitated to him, each attracted by that facet of the legend that lured him most.

Hemingway was a warm and sweet guy, a soft touch for a sad story. Violent, physical, rough people liked him. He seemed defenceless against the inroads of such characters, and to tell the truth, in many such types he found the kind of companions he admired. There were bound to be fights; and in all fairness, where there's smoke there must be fire, Hemingway did have his wild, abrasive side; physical action of all kinds had always been a real part of his philosophy of living.

Despite the fact that he drank more and more as time passed and was beginning to put on weight, he kept himself in fine physical condition. He never hesitated to accept combat if there was no other way out.

So the legend grew. To the near exclusion of everything so different in his character, he became famous as the brawling, quick-fisted, hard-drinking dean of American writers. His press notices were always good. He got lots and lots of publicity. Hemingway was always good copy and nothing was overlooked. The public ate it up. The somewhat bewildered and resentful "intellectuals" stoked the fires.

In life Hemingway tended to play the "hero" role. He just didn't invent for his stories and books. All of this infuriated the so-called aesthetes and many of the critics—the whole tribe that has the power to put the seal of approval or disapproval on an artist. Not content with trying to understand and judge his work for what it was, they insisted on looking at it in the light of the legend. The work proved the truth of the legend, so they said, and the legend proved the worthlessness of the work.

What they refused to see was that here was a man who in life and in work had to get his teeth into the meat of living. Instead of taking an idea and chewing on it like a cow with a cud, he insisted on testing it against life itself. He insisted on feeling and tasting and touching the real thing.

No one was aware—or if they were they preferred to overlook it in favor of the juicier public antics—of the long grinding hours of labor he put in at his writing, trying, always trying, to beat the words into submission and to make them say what he wished.

No one was particularly interested either—it didn't make very exciting copy—in Hemingway's enormous cultural background. Following a lifelong custom, he read constantly and widely. Everything was fuel for his avid mind—the daily columns, essays, history, military memoirs, the eternal classics. Hemingway could, and would, talk penetratingly on anything under the sun if given half a chance.

He loved great art of any kind. As he put it, "I'm a sucker for a fine painting." Among his most prized possessions, along with his guns, were his paintings. Cézanne, Degas, Goya, as well as Picasso, whom he had known well in Paris, were among his favorite painters.

He prepared a list of his favorite books (no one was much interested in it!), the ones he would "rather read again for the first time than be assured of a million-dollar annual income." The list included Emily Bronte's *Wuthering Heights*, W. H. Hudson's *Far Away and Long Ago*, Mark Twain's *Huckleberry Finn* (he considered Twain *the* great American writer), Anderson's *Winesburg, Ohio*, George Moore's *Hail and Farewell*, James Joyce's *Dubliners*, Thomas Mann's *Buddenbrooks*, Stendhal's *The Red and The Black* and *The Charter-House of Parma*, Tolstoy's *War and Peace*, Dumas Père's *Queen Margot*, Flaubert's *Madame Bovary*, Dostoevsky's *The Brothers Karamazov*, Turgenev's *A Sportsman's Sketches*, and de Maupassant's *House of Madame Tellier*.

Hemingway also insisted that his sons learn to read and to love books. One of his favorites was the *Memoires* of General Jean Marbot. According to John (the Bumby of those youthful Paris days), "He made me read it too." And then, so typical of Hemingway, he also insisted that son John learn to box.

After *The Sun Also Rises* was published, Hemingway lived on for a while longer in Paris, where he started a new book.

In 1927, three weeks after his divorce from Hadley, he was married again, to Pauline Pfeiffer and shortly afterwards they came home, this time permanently, to America. They moved to Key West, Florida, where he soon became the sleepy little village's most prominent citizen. In Key West he finished *A Farewell to Arms,* which was published in 1929.

Those who insisted on making the myth of the Hemingway legend come to life had a field day. Here was proof positive. The apostle of blood and violence had at last come into his own. The book was based mainly on Hemingway's war experiences on the Italian front and his journalistic days in Asia Minor. It was filled with the thunder and the pace and the suffering of war. According to the detractors, its heroes were simply bloodthirsty men. The detractors didn't look deeply enough. Those who were looking for the violence of war, to prove something about Hemingway they already believed, found it.

The superb artistry of the book, however, and its competence, brought it tremendous acclaim—both critical and popular. The prose flowed so swiftly and the spare, crystalline language was so compelling that nearly everyone was caught up in it—willingly or not. The real values in the book were apt to be overlooked in the spell cast by the sheer strength of the writing.

"The dignity of movement of an iceberg," Hemingway once said, "is due to only one-eighth of it being above water."

And so with *A Farewell to Arms.* People tend to be blinded by the genius of its architecture. They feel that this is what gives the book dignity. In part this is true, but the vast bulk of meaning lying underneath the superb flow of the story is where the reader must really search.

The apostle of blood and violence! Such nonsense! Of his experiences in the war about which he now wrote, he said, "I remember feeling so awful about the first war that I was unable to write about it for ten years!"

In *A Farewell to Arms* Hemingway has his hero say, "I was always embarrassed by the words sacred, glorious, and sacrifice and the expression in vain. . . . I had seen nothing sacred and the things that were glorious had no glory and the sacrifices were like the stockyards at Chicago if nothing was done with the meat except to bury it . . ."

Hemingway knew full well there is no glory in a torn and smashed human body, or in the loss of love. There is no dignity in babbling shell shock. He could not stand hypocrisy; he could not tolerate the high sounding words used to describe the meaningless blood bath that is war.

In this novel, along with his other books, as well as the some 50 odd short stories he published up through 1939 alone, there runs, glinting like flecks of light on silver, over and over again the theme: Violence for the sake of violence has no meaning in life.

Hemingway considered life a tragedy—death was its inevitable end. Along the road however, there was plenty of opportunity for action, plenty of opportunity to put up a good courageous performance, and this was all that mattered. His heroes were often rough, and tough, and there is plenty of the language and excitement of the gutter. But never simply for its own sake. There was always meaning there for those with the patience to look, and for those who were not spellbound by the perfection of the surface structure.

There is actually little violence in his writing. He used

just what is necessary to make his point, and even this was frequently minimized. Direct scenes of action are often merely talked about and commented upon by his characters, rather than acted out.

During the Key West years while Hemingway was revising *A Farewell To Arms,* his second son, Patrick, was born. The birth nearly took the life of Pauline.

In the midst of bringing life to his book; in the midst of the harrowing birth of his son, death also came to Hemingway. It shook him to his bones and put to the supreme test his belief that cowardice in the face of the blows of life was one of the greatest sins. A man, so he felt, lived his life fully, fought with courage and to the best of his ability the problems of each day. A test of manhood was the degree to which he confronted the problems living brought to him. In Oak Park, Hemingway's father committed suicide. In an upstairs bedroom the Doctor took his own life with a revolver.

A sorrowing son went to Oak Park to clear up the family affairs. Sorrowing, yes, and yet Hemingway must have at this moment hated his father with all his being for doing this. When a man's time came to die, he faced death calmly. In the meantime he lived his life with bravery.

A glimpse into Hemingway's heart at this tragic moment appears in one of the Nick Adams stories called "Fathers and Sons." Nick sorrowfully hints that his own father, Dr. Adams, has taken his own life. ". . . Nick had loved him very much and for a long time. Now, knowing how it had all been, even remembering the earliest times before things had gone badly was not good remembering. If he wrote it he could get rid of it. He had gotten rid of many things by writing them. But it was still too early for that. There were still too many people. So he decided to think of something else. There was nothing to do about his father and he had thought it all through many times. The handsome job the undertaker had done on his father's face had not blurred in his mind and all the rest of it was quite clear, including the responsibilities. He had complimented the undertaker. The undertaker had been both proud and smugly pleased. But it was not the undertaker that had given him that last face. The undertaker had only made certain dashingly executed repairs of doubtful artistic merit. The face had been making itself and being made for a long time. It had modelled fast in the last three years. It was a good story but there were still too many people alive for him to write it."

How poignantly does the grief and the numbed agony of the son come through in this simple expression of love, the simple yet unearthly clarity of the description of his dead father's face.

Hemingway faced up to his responsibilities as the eldest son in the family. He did the necessary things and returned to Key West to his work.

Part of the Hemingway legend states that he earned millions of dollars from his books and never willingly parted with a penny of it. When his father died, he privately set up a series of trust funds to provide for the education of his little brother and his sisters.

One of Hemingway's characters in *The Sun Also Rises* says: "Nobody ever lives their life all the way up except bullfighters."

On his first postwar trip to Paris, he had been interested

in bullfighting. This interest was twofold. First of all, he was very much concerned with developing his vision to see what he saw, and not what he thought he saw. From this, his concern was to sharpen his literary tools to meet the challenge of the unique and terribly moving spectacle. First he had to understand what he saw, and then write about it.

Hemingway has written great stories about boxing. He knew a lot about the sport. He wrote fine stories about other sports as well: fishing and hunting. But to him, the great hero, the one who played out his role the closest to the way it actually is in life was the *torero*, the bullfighter.

The second reason for his consuming interest in bullfighting was that he instinctively felt there must be something more to it than the general opinion held by most Anglo-Saxons. Most of them react in something like revulsion, bringing to the spectacle a love of fair play, a dislike of cruelty to animals. Hemingway was determined to find out what lay at the bottom of the Spanish national pastime.

For Hemingway, death was very near the center of his work and of his personal philosophy. "All stories, if continued far enough, end in death, and he is no true story-teller who would keep that from you," he once wrote.

Hemingway wrote: "Someone with English blood has written: 'Life is real, life is earnest, and the grave is not its goal.' And where did they bury him? and what became of the reality and the earnestness? The people of Castile have great common sense. They could not produce a poet who would write a line like that. They know death is the unescapable reality, the one thing any man may be sure of; the only security . . . ."

Earlier he had written, "I am not going to apologize for bullfighting. It is a survival of the days of the Roman Coliseum. But it does need some explanation. Bullfighting is not a sport. It was never supposed to be. It is a tragedy. A very great tragedy. The tragedy is the death of the bull. . . ."

In 1926 Hemingway wrote to his editor, Maxwell Perkins, that he wanted to do a book on bullfighting. Not an apology, nor a do-it-yourself textbook. He wanted to do something that would almost be the bullfight itself, that would lay bare whatever was beneath the panoply and the near mystical ritual.

Off and on, during many trips to Spain, the book was finally finished and brought out in January, 1932. He called it *Death in the Afternoon*. The critics, of course, tore the book apart. It was gory, sadistic, degenerate. It glorified cold-blooded murder, made sport out of torturing a helpless animal. The legend-builders had a field day.

Those who read carefully, with an open mind, learned a great deal about Spain and the nature of a spectacle the origins of which go further back even than the written memory of mankind. They also learned something about themselves and the implications inherent in the world in which they live. They learned that the essentials of the Spanish philosophy of life were *love, death,* and *eternity,* applied to all men, everywhere, in or out of a bullring.

Hemingway watched, and he wrote over long years to try to capture in words and portray what to him was the true meaning in a bullfight. Very quickly he found out he had tackled a great deal more than he bargained for.

What eventually it came to mean to him, he put down in *Death in the Afternoon.*

He said that a bullfight is a tragedy. Like all tragedies, it has three acts. In essence, they are the offering and the refusal of death; the recognition of it, then rebellion and struggle against it; and finally, the inevitable acceptance.

In Act I, after the matador has made his preliminary passes, the horse comes out, with the picadors and their silly little lances. This is the comic part. The horse and the picadors are the comedians. Keeping in mind that Hemingway was searching for deeper meanings, and forgetting our own natural love for animals and our distaste at seeing them hurt, it can only be comic that such characters could offer death to a powerful fighting bull. The bull disdainfully rejects the comedy. He often kills or badly wounds his despised fellow-actors.

In Act II the plot gets more serious. The bull rebels, fights against death. The bandilleros, digging deep with their small dart-like javelins, injure and wound the bull. He becomes more wary, highly dangerous, sobered. He has come to realize this "game" is being played for keeps. He aims every horn stroke, calculates each rush, concentrates his hatred on individual objects—first the bandilleros and then the matador himself.

In Act III, at the climactic moment of killing, there is a sense of doom, of inevitability—a profundity of feeling that transfers itself from the ring to the spectators. Everyone rebels against death. Vicariously the spectators have exchanged places with the matador and themselves administer the death-dealing stroke. "When a man is still in rebellion against death he has the pleasure in making himself one of the god-like attributes: that of giving it."

The hero is the matador, the man of action. The grace with which he plays his part, the performance he puts up, determines the success or failure of the real life drama that has been acted out in the ring. In the same way the performance man puts up as we go through life determines our own success or failure. The end, death, in a way is unimportant. It is inevitable and all are equal before it. In the drama the bull is not forgotten. Bulls resist death, just as men do, and a great fighting bull is much admired. He puts up a struggle, a good act, but when the end comes, he faces the inevitable with courage.

There are those who say that bullfights are "fixed" in the sense that they are *really* not dangerous for the men. This is not so. Hemingway says, and as always, reports truthfully: "In sixteen fights I saw there were only two in which there was no one badly hurt."

The famous American bullfighter, a Brooklyn boy named Sidney Franklin, was a close friend of Hemingway's. Franklin was one of the all-time great matadors and Hemingway's admiration for him was tremendous. Franklin helped greatly in supplying material for *Death in the Afternoon*.

"He was the first American who spoke to me intelligently about bullfighting," said Franklin. "Other Americans tried to tell me they knew more about the business than I did. Ernest let me do the talking. I found we both thought the same. Our minds ran along the same track. . . . He used to stand behind the *barrera* [the fence around the ring] and watch me fight. I would fight for Ernest, to solve the problems for his bullfight book—*Death in the Afternoon*. When I was on tour, he doubled up in a room with me, and we'd spend the whole night talking about fights, techniques, styles, and bulls. He'd tell me things I didn't know myself."

When *Death in the Afternoon* was published, the United

[*112*]

States and all of Europe were clamped in the grip of a dark economic depression. There were breadlines, souplines, people without jobs, hunger marches on Washington, charges and counter-charges of Communism, and all sorts of other serious problems.

The world couldn't have cared less at that moment about a book on the intricacies and the mystique of bullfighting. Hemingway, carpers said, was a literary irresponsible. He should be turning his talents to the important things, writing about the big social questions instead of this fiddle-faddle on killing bulls, this make-believe "problem." But Hemingway wrote and published his book. To him it was not a bloodless abstraction. To him it was a slice of life, it was an attempt to give meaning to one aspect of those deep and powerful currents that carry us on to our inevitable end—the grave.

Furthermore, the book was out of his own experience. He was not a bullfighter. After the original nearly disastrous attempt at Pamplona, he had decided to leave it to others more nimble than he. But he did know the sensation. He did know what it was to be on foot and face a ton of furious, agile bone and muscle.

As Hemingway said, "a thousand years makes economics silly and a work of art endures forever."

Death in the Afternoon may not all be great art, although the last chapter dealing with impressions of Spain comes very close to it. Nevertheless, this strange book written by a man from Oak Park, Illinois—a man on whose mind and body had been imprinted the attitudes and beliefs of his Midwestern, middle-class upbringing—is still very much alive, and very likely may be for some time to come.

[*113*]

Chapter **8**

Those Distant Green Hills

T he years Hemingway spent in Key West were happy, vital, and busy years: a time of growth, of hard work, so filled with activity of all kinds that one wonders where the time came from. The big, old-fashioned two story house Hemingway lived in half hidden in palms and poincianas was not the "luxurious villa" that legend insists upon, but it was at the core of Hemingway's life.

With Pauline and the boys—soon there were two of them —he spent long hours on the beaches. The climate and the scenery of this southernmost spit of land in the United States might have been monotonous to some. To the Hemingways it was a constantly changing panorama of excitement and adventure. The sea was never distant; it was their continual companion. To the wary observer, and soon the family was as alert as Hemingway himself, the seasons as they came and went, the cycles of sun, tides, skies, stars and clouds, were clear cut and powerful influences. The "wonders of the deep"—the lives of those creatures, great and small, peopling the vast ocean— were thrilling and exciting, a never ending source of adventure.

And for Hemingway always there was the work. The tapping of the typewriter and the scratch of pencil on paper from the upstairs study never ceased. As regular as the lapping of the sea on the sands, it began each day at dawn or a little before and continued until after noon.

But life was far from sedentary. Hemingway loved change and motion and action. They stimulated and renewed him. "Don't do anything too bloody long" was never more true than during the years at Key West. Visitors came and went in a steady stream. The staccato rat-a-tat-tat of a punching bag and the solid thump of leather on leather echoed daily from the ring up the street. At night there was drinking in the little bars about town, and much tall talk. Key West was filled with fine, big talk, almost always of the sea and the strange things that happened upon it. Merchant seamen, fishermen, smugglers, men from nearby Navy bases all added their bit.

Hemingway and Pauline roamed the Western United States hunting and fishing. He bagged bear and moose in the great forests of the North, antelope on the plains, and sheep and goats along the stupendous slopes of the Rockies. He exulted in his prowess and reputation as a big game fisherman. Tired of renting boats, he was able at last to afford a boat of his own. A trim boat constructed exactly to his specifications was built in an old New England shipyard. She was a beauty and had everything—even two engines, one for high speeds to get where he wanted in a hurry and the other, much smaller, to deliver the steady, snail's pace used in trolling. Hemingway christened his boat the *Pilar,* after a much loved shrine in Spain. She was a shrine to him, and a haven.

On the *Pilar* he spent long hours at sea, fishing, studying the sea's moods, its colors, its effects on those who ventured

Fishing from the Pilar *was always a welcome way to relax.*

upon it. They sailed majestically through a school of gigantic whales; he observed that rarest of phenomena, marlin mating. He learned what it meant when a school of flying fish went dancing and skittering over the swells, or when the schools of dolphin, the long lines undulating like sea serpents, accompanied the *Pilar* to the Gulf Stream. He discovered a new species of fish, a rosefish, that was named after him and in honor of his love of the sea, *Neomarinthe hemingwayi.*

Often he crossed the 90 miles over to Havana to fish the Gulf Stream from that side. He rented a room in the Hotel Ambos Mundos, overlooking the harbor, the seawall, and the ancient battlements. When his absences from Key West were long ones he slept and worked there. He kept this room for years.

Even though living now permanently in the United States, Hemingway was still in a sense an expatriate. He found no inspiration or stimulation in the mainstream of artistic and literary life in New York. Occasional trips to the nightclubs of the big city were all that he needed. He found laughter, good talk, and much to drink there; but when the trips were over he returned invariably to the sanctuary of sea and beach, sky and ocean.

Always the legend grew. His antics in the bars in Havana and in the nightclubs and gyms of New York were all that his critics saw or cared about. They were not interested in the long hours of writing and reading, the picnics with his family on the beaches. Life beneath the great Caribbean sky, the solace and the rejuvenation he found on the sea, these things had no part in the Hemingway legend that was fed to the public.

But there still remained other huge worlds that he wanted to see. There were other skies, other hills, other big game he wanted to shoot. In 1922, during the first years in Paris, he had published his earliest known book review, about a novel *Batoula*, by a young Negro writer named René Maran. The book cut to the core of the sham of French colonial policy as it traced the life and death of a native African chieftain. The book created a stir, but what impressed the young artist Hemingway most was its clear, truthful presentation of African life from a native's point of view. Maran must have been a writer after Hemingway's heart.

He speaks of the book as though he were declaiming a credo of his own: "You smell the smells of the village, you eat its food, you see the white man as the black man sees him, and after you have lived in the village you die there. That is all there is to the story, but when you have read it, you have been Batouala [the native chief], and that means it is a great novel."

The review has long been forgotten, but the book stirred in Hemingway's heart a flame of interest in Africa that continued to live. No doubt many times in southern Spain or France he must have looked even further to the south toward the dark continent, lying like a thin smudge on the horizon. The desire to walk and hunt through its green hills never left him.

In 1933 Pauline and Ernest left Key West. They passed through Marseilles in November and a short time later crossed over to Africa to start what was to be a four-month safari through the big game country.

He wrote a book about this trip called *The Green Hills of Africa*. It is by no means the greatest of his books, nor is it the most famous. It does have, however, a very special quality that sets it apart from everything else he has written, or for that matter, from anything anyone else has ever written on the subject. *The Green Hills of Africa* is also the book in which the real Hemingway comes closest to the surface. Here perhaps, it is easiest to get an inkling of what he was really like.

Always it is difficult to know another human being. Each person's credo, his reason for living, his approach to life —all those things that make us what we really are—are different. Some people are profound; some are shallow. The task, as Hemingway himself says, "is to understand, not to judge." This is not easy. What is inside most people is buried very deeply. It is always obscured by those surface things that the world at large uses to make its too easy judgments. A personality might be compared to an onion. Layer after layer must be peeled off to get at what is inside. And, as with peeling an onion, the eyes of the peeler more often than not are apt to blur and fill with tears before he gets anywhere near the core.

The Green Hills is primarily about a land and the wild life that lives in it. There are people, of course, but not too many of them. They are not too complex and they do not occupy the center of the stage. The star of the show is the writer—Hemingway. He has top billing. Perhaps it is for this reason—drawn as he is in bright clarity against the world of nature, with very little competition from other human beings—that he shines forth so clearly.

First off, strictly as a travel book, filled with excitement, the book is magnificent. Hemingway's clear way of looking at things with wide-open, unbiased eyes, his selection of evocative details that heighten and give meaning to a larger and more blurred background have never been put to more telling use.

There is none of the romantic, pseudo-poetic nonsense in the travelogue style of "Once again as the setting sun drops beneath the sea we bid farewell to the happy natives of Shangri-La." Nor is the book constructed of the dead bones of a description of travel merely listing points of interest and putting stars beside the more important ones.

For Hemingway art was the truth and the truth art. Through him we see the truth; perhaps some day it may be called great art. True, truth, truly—these are words we constantly find, and feel, in his work.

In another story, "Soldier's Home," we find a clear and beautiful expression of Hemingway's distaste for the false. Krebs, the soldier, has returned home long after all the other veterans. He had been drafted late. He had a need to talk, but no one wanted to hear about his experiences. The people had already heard too many stories. "Krebs found that to be listened to at all he had to lie, and after he had done this twice he, too, had a reaction against the war and against talking about it. A distaste for everything that had happened to him in the war set in because of the lies he had told. All of the times that had been able to make him feel cool and clear inside himself when he thought of them; the times so long back when he had done the one thing, the only thing for a man to do, easily and naturally, when he might have done something else, now lost their cool, valuable quality and then were lost themselves. . . . Krebs acquired the nausea in regard to experience that is the result of untruth or exaggeration. . . . In this way he lost everything."

In Hemingway's life too, in spite of the legend, truth was a credo, a way of existence, in matters large and small. He once implied to a friend, in a convivial mood, that he had gone to Princeton. Later, unable even to live with this, he said, "I always say I have been to Princeton at such times, because I think I was jealous of Scott Fitzgerald!"

This scrupulous, almost fanatical honesty is at the root of Hemingway's character and of his writing. In *The Green Hills of Africa* this dedication to the way things really were causes the sky, the water, the animals, the birds and the natives to project themselves from the pages of the book. Thy take on the dimensions and meanings of life itself. The impression is inescapable.

A lion, "looking yellow and heavy-headed and enormous against a scrubby-looking tree in a patch of orchard bush . . ." moves to the left "on a run, a strange, heavy-shouldered, foot-swinging cat run."

A hyena comes "suddenly wedge-headed and stinking out of the high grass by a *donga*" and lopes away across "the brown plain, looking back, mongrel-dog-smart in the face."

Flamingoes rise on long angular wings, with pumping skinny legs into the sun over Lake Manyara "making the whole horizon of the lake pink".

Or a sky "full of locusts" passes overhead and the daylight flickers through them "like an old cinema film."

There are these and much much more. The reader learns how it is to wait at a salt lick or at a baited trap for game. He catches the feel of coming home across the plain to the camp at the end of a day, the taste of food. The natives—gun-bearers, camp boys, guides—all spring to sudden life and become real people.

Hemingway loved this land dearly. "I knew a good country when I saw one," he said. "Here there was game, plenty of birds, and I liked the natives. Here I could shoot and fish. That, and writing and reading, and seeing pictures, was all I cared about doing. And I could remember all the pictures. Other things I liked to watch but they were what I liked to do."

Hemingway went to Africa as a hunter, a killer, if you like, make no bones about it. He enjoyed the thrill of pitting his own courage and skill against that of other living, equally deadly creatures. He shot his share of animals and birds—for food and for trophies.

He wrote about it superbly. The sweat springs to the reader's hands, and beneath his fingers he feels the hot, oily walnut and steel of the rifle as he stands tensed, peering into the tall grass. In that grass is the most lethal of all Africa's creatures—a huge gold and black leopard, with canary-yellow eyes. Did the quick shot miss, did it kill him, or is he just wounded? The reader wonders and hears the beat of his own heart thumping steadily through the words and lines leaping out at him from the pages.

Yes, Hemingway went to Africa after big game. Because he was also a writer, an artist, he found far more than this beneath the sights of his guns.

He began his safari in excitement and anticipation. He ended it in wonder and delight. There is a primeval quality about these boundless plains and hills of Africa. They echo to the roar of great, fearsome beasts. The skies are filled with the squawk and whir of strange birds. The earth trembles beneath the thundering hooves of animals so numerous they are counted by the millions upon millions. Yes, there is a quality to these hills of Africa. It's the way the earth must have been in the days of creation, when all was fresh and young and when all creatures were at one in the struggle for life, for survival . . . and equal in the ultimate surrender to death.

When Hemingway wandered with his party, with his gun-bearers, or alone, he must have caught this. He must have felt as the first man felt when he too wandered for the first time on this beautiful earth—solitary, small, and insignificant before the majesty of the land, filled with awe.

Hemingway could not have felt as a stranger, an interloper. He had ever been a participater; all his writing sprang from nature—from what was alive. A man, he believed, must enter into life, must never simply sit on the sidelines and look the situation over. In Africa, life of all kinds was so vital, and so urgent, he could not have felt less than a part of it, could not have done less than respond with his whole being to it.

In such a situation, any man, if his vision is not totally dulled, arrives at a personal philosophy. When Hemingway arrived in these lovely, living, breathing beautiful hills, he already had one. He brought it with him. But his response was such to Africa that it leaps out at you from the book. As Hemingway wanders beneath the vast, arching skies, and across Africa's endless land, the reader feels that he is humbled, almost overwhelmed.

He seems to be a naturalist, but not one of those fuddy-duddy classroom specimens whose chief business is discovery, or description, or counting noses. He is the kind of a naturalist that is absorbed wholly into the powerful flow of life itself, a part of it, and not a strange being from another planet who merely spies on the creatures walking the earth with him.

Hemingway's concern seems to be with the massive ebb and flow of the primary motivating forces, the basic primal forces that shape and affect us all. He is fascinated by the interweaving, the complexity of all life, including his own . . . because *he is a part*.

Even the dullest clod of a man must sometimes look at himself in the mirror and wonder who he really is. He must ponder where and how he fits into some kind of an overall pattern or scheme. Out of such wonderings and ponderings have sprung man's great religions, his philosophies—all the things that set man as a species apart from others. Perhaps the neuroses and the vast tensions of today stem partly from the fact that too many men nowadays are willing to leave such considerations to scholars and professors. It is the business of all men to think about these matters if they are to survive.

The great mysteries, the processes of survival, are the same for all creatures on this earth. All life is like a pyramid. Men's lives, whether they know it or not, or whether they like it or not, are a part of this pyramid formed of living things.

Upon the bottom of any pond are pastured the tiny grazing animals—pollywogs, snails, microscopic organisms. In the unbelievable prodigality of nature, each one of them will produce millions of descendants.

Just above these peaceful grazers are the little creatures of prey—nymphs, crayfish, minnows—all of them ravenous and vicious as hungry tigers. The same fate awaits them as awaits the placid little creatures below them. They too are destined to vanish into the stomachs of still larger creatures.

At the top of the pyramid, fewer in number, but far more deadly, more efficient in this business of survival, are the greater creatures, including man himself. But necessity presses just as sternly upon man as it does upon the smaller creatures. Problems of food and population are just the same. Life for man is just as harsh, just as inexorable. His increased consciousness, his appreciations, his awareness do not absolve him from the harsh laws that govern all the living.

To man sometimes life looks so terrible that he can find no peace, save in faith, like that of an albatross sailing serenely on the billows of wind, or like a doe leaving her helpless fawn asleep in faith against the terrors of the night while she goes to graze in the moonlight.

Man is safe only so long as he believes in life itself. He must not expect any special intervention for himself. As Hemingway saw most clearly, there can be no final quarter for men as *individuals* when death approaches. Life continues but individual man must die. In the sweep and power of its mass, life is irrepressible and eternal. Individually it is frail enough, heaven knows, and as no man knows, how immortal. There is nothing pleasant about all this. It is more to man's liking to eat than to be eaten. But even kings come to dust and to what awaits all of us beyond.

Hemingway knew this. Death is always very near to the center of his writing. His detractors say that death was his theme, his only theme. And then, getting a little Freudian, they say he wrote about it because of his morbid fear of it.

Such nonsense! *Life* was Hemingway's theme. The measure of a man was the grace with which he lived life, clear out to the end. Since death does await all men, this knowledge also plays a part in the way men live their lives. It can't be otherwise, and here is the kernel of the truth of Ernest Hemingway, out of which, as usual, quite a different legend has been fabricated.

In *The Green Hills of Africa* comes a subtle change in the way Hemingway the writer thought and felt. He had come as a killer, but he no longer stalked his game ruthlessly with cruel, blazing guns. He continued to hunt, of course, but there is the feeling, as time passes, that he descended *downward* from his level as a modern man to that of the animals and of the land about him. He is no longer merely a *killer*. He has become a *hunter*. Hunting his own prey as they in turn hunt theirs, he no longer seems a transgressor, an alien.

Throughout the latter part of the book, bagging a kudu becomes an obsession with Hemingway. As the hunt progresses, he becomes more and more at one with his quarry. He shares the heat, the dirt, the suffering, the uncertainty throughout the flight and chase, with the animal itself. When he finally kills the kudu, and, weary and tired, squats on his haunches beside him, his words are almost a eulogy: "I looked at him, big, long-legged, a smooth gray with the white stripes and the great, curling, sweeping horns . . . and I stooped over and touched him to try to believe it."

He'd got his kudu. It seemed almost too good to be true.

It is a eulogy, but more nearly a lament. The reader is ready to forgive Hemingway for killing the great animal. What is more important, he is almost ready to believe that the kudu also has forgiven him.

In the irreparable losses brought about by death, even in the laying down of one's own life, there is only one single, bleak thing to sustain man: the courage that comes with the knowledge that it is shared by *all living things*; that mortal experience is brief and that its end is always the same.

Hemingway knew it and this is what he wrote about.

In addition to *The Green Hills* two other magnificent pieces of work came out of Hemingway's African experience.

They are short stories, but they are among his finest works.

During the course of the safari, Hemingway picked up that scourge of life in unsanitary parts of the world, dysentery. He fought it but finally was forced to give in. He was flown out for hospital treatment and after a short period of treatment was able to rejoin his party. While in the plane flying past the snowy peak of Mt. Kilimanjaro, the germ of one of these stories began to turn and twist in his mind. He was gravely ill; possibly the sight of the distant icy mountain, like an impossible path to climb, suggested the idea: the death of a writer before his work is done. What came out of his ponderings, "The Snows of Kilimanjaro," is one of his most successful stories.

The main character Harry has come to Africa. He lies gravely ill with gangrene. Harry suffers mentally as well as physically. He is a writer, but he could be any man who has sold himself out for quick and easy money, fame, and adulation. The loss of his integrity is like a sword in his heart. Time is short. He senses the approach of death. Anxiously he awaits the arrival of the rescue plane to take him to Nairobi where he can get proper medical treatment.

After Harry has spent a night of agony, the plane arrives. It takes off. Eventually it dawns on Harry that something is wrong. Ahead, on a level with the plane he sees the incredible, craggy peak of Kilimanjaro, "wide as all the world." He realizes they are off course: they are *not* going to Nairobi. During the night, at the camp, Helen, Harry's wife awakens and calls to her husband. He does not answer. He is dead. The flight had been a dying dream. The plane had never come.

All that is implied in this beautiful story was once expressed by another American writer in quite a different way.

Henry James said: "It is glory to have been tested, to have had our little quality and cast our little spell. A second chance—*that's* the delusion. There never was to be but one. We work in the dark, we do what we can, we give what we have. Our doubt is our passion and our passion is our task."

Comparisons between writers are often pointless. Hemingway himself had no stomach for it. It is interesting, however, to examine certain characteristics of good writers. It would be difficult to find two men more dissimilar on the surface than Hemingway and James. Their subject matter was different, their locales were different, their characters different, their interests were widely separated. Even their styles were worlds apart. One was spare, stripped, terse. The other's was embellished, intricate, with "asides" and directions for the reader. Yet, they have something in common. A scene of James, if stripped down to its bones, is not much different than if Hemingway had written it. In each there are the hypersensitive, acute writer's eye and feel. In each there is the effort to get to the basic essentials, the essence, the distillation that comes out of the icy, objective contemplation of tangled human affairs. Hemingway called this the effort to see "how a thing truly was."

The other story that came out of Hemingway's African trip is called "The Short Happy Life of Francis Macomber." It too is concerned with the loss of integrity by a man. Francis Macomber has sold himself out to an unscrupulous woman. He is demeaned to the point where he cannot continue to live unless he regains his lost manhood. This he does. When his wife sees what has happened she is unable to stand the loss of her "slave" and so in final degradation, she kills him. The short, happy life of Francis Macomber has lasted about thirty minutes.

In this story, beneath all its surface excitement, Hemingway again expresses the theme that once a man's integrity is gone, something vital and precious has been lost. There is no second chance. No matter how man struggles he cannot get back what he has so carelessly thrown away.

In Africa, Hemingway's adventures were not confined to the land alone. Never a man to pass up the chance to wet a line, he chartered a boat and did some big game fishing along the coast of the continent.

The expedition was not a success, but a comic failure. The engine of the launch chose to quit invariably at the crucial moments. They caught nothing. With memories perhaps of the more reliable *Pilar* in mind, Hemingway quit in disgust.

He and Pauline were back in Key West by April of 1934. Already dark clouds were gathering over a land that Hemingway loved dearly, Spain. He read the signs clearly. The next years were to be sorrowful and deeply scarring ones. The legend, the myth was to grow enormously. Hemingway also grew enormously in stature as a man.

Chapter 9

Tragedy in Spain

Hemingway has been harshly accused of being or *not* being, just about everything under the sun. One of the sins his detractors charge him with is that he was irresponsible in his literature. He was apolitical.

What they mean is that he should have taken it upon himself to expose causes. He should have used his talents to help clean up some of the world's various evil messes. He should have used his skills in the cause of good government, social justice, labor unions, kindness to animals, free school lunches for children, or whatever at the moment seemed most important.

Many good writers have done this. Hemingway chose not to. In steering clear of such questions, no matter how large or important they might loom at the moment, he was in very good company. The greatest artists that mankind has produced have in general preferred to probe away at the age-old problems that are *always* with us. Good and evil, love and hatred, joy and sorrow, life and death, courage and cowardice, truth and falsehood, to name a few.

To Hemingway, these were the basic questions. They were

the ancient facts of life that have bedeviled men since the beginning of time, regardless of the kind of government or social system in vogue at the moment. These were the things that made men tick, that needed to be explored, understood.

There had been one exception: Fascism. Fascism enraged Hemingway. He was writing and preaching against it way back in the days when the rest of the world seemed to admire it. Hemingway is known to have made but one public speech in his life. This was in 1937 before the general assembly of the Writers' Congress in New York.

He told an overflow crowd: "Fascism is a lie told by bullies. A writer who will not lie cannot live and work under Fascism." As the whole world was to find out to its sorrow later on, he was right. And he might well have substituted the word "man" for writer. As far back as 1931 Hemingway had watched uneasily while the political pot bubbled and stewed in Spain. By 1936, the explosion took place. The long black spell of Fascism, which he hated, fell across Spain, across a land and people he loved.

Courage is nothing new to Spaniards, nor is violent, mass death. Spaniards have died in arms in the Netherlands, in Peru, in Mexico, in Morocco. They have perished from fever and in front of the guns in the Philippines, in Cuba. They have died at home too, the young and the old, from hunger and disease and overwork in factories, on the vast *haciendas* which they did not own, and in the squalid village huts, which they did not own either.

Humble, submissive, even in the presence of constant death, the tragedy of the Spanish people is that they have always died in vain. There never was even a national anthem that they could call their own—just the Royal March. In Spain there was never a blood bath in a righteous upheaval from below against the oppression of tradition. In Spain there never had been a French Revolution, never a Fourth of July and a war fought to ultimate liberty. Until the 1930's Spain was one of the most medieval countries in the world.

In 1931, the Spanish Republic was formed, peaceably, or reasonably so, as these things go. Hemingway watched as the best brains of the land wrote the new constitution. He rejoiced as they tried to guarantee freedom for all Spaniards. He cheered as they tried even to outlaw death—violent death. There was to be no such thing as capital punishment in Spain any more. This land had had enough of such things.

To the crimson and gold banner of Spain was added a stripe of purple, the purple of the pennant of old Castile. The purple of permanganate—one of the strongest antiseptics known—was added to the blood and pus. Along with the crowd Hemingway cheered: *"Que vive el permanganato!"* "Long live permanganate!" The crowds cheered themselves hoarse.

For about two years, it looked as though the permanganate might work, and that all the Spanish dead down through the centuries might not have died in vain. The Republic started clearing out the vast debris of the past, reviving the best of the old values, and building to the future. But the debris was far from inert. The Republic was building on sand, truly castles in Spain.

In July, 1936, the movement of revolt started in certain sections of the officer corps of the Army. Men who wanted freedom but freedom only for themselves, not for the *canalla,* as they called the people, took matters into their own hands. The struggle was on.

The great democracies of the world—France, Britain, the United States, proclaimed policies of strict neutrality. Hands off to insult no one, and to hope that the fire would burn itself out. This row in Spain was none of their business. It should be settled between the Spaniards themselves. This was an honest position (if the assumption is made that the struggle of men for liberty anywhere is not the business of free men everywhere), but it wasn't very clear thinking, as time was to show.

The Fascist powers, Germany and Italy, did not hesitate. This was a struggle which *they* understood. They came to the aid of oppression with everything in their power. In a battle of freedom versus slavery, humanity versus inhumanity, there was no question of *their* position.

Nor was there any question in Ernest Hemingway's mind. This was a struggle which he too understood. Clearly he saw it was a battle for freedom and deserving the best from those who believed in freedom. Even more chillingly, he saw that it was only the curtain raiser for another world-wide bloodletting. He felt that any small bit he could do now might help to stop what was to come. He jumped in with both feet and fists.

His first act was to borrow $40,000 to buy ambulances and medical supplies for the Loyalists. "I'd like to send a lot of ambulances," he said, "because you can't have a war without people getting hurt. If people help the Loyalists, others charge them right away with being Communists. I can't see any other reason why the American Red Cross has not sent help. It's like a guy lying hurt in the middle of the street with lots of nice people walking by and refusing to help him pick himself up because they're afraid of being sued." Naive perhaps, but honest. . . .

Forty thousand dollars is a lot of money and it represented a very sizeable lien against his future. In order to start paying off the loan he went to Spain as a war correspondent for the North American Newspaper Alliance. He sailed for Spain with his friend the bullfighter Sidney Franklin. At the Spanish border with France, came the first shock of reality and the first real glimpse of the ramifications and the immensity of the struggle lying ahead. From Toulouse, he wrote, "On the day on which the American State Department, following its policy of strictest neutrality, refused Sidney Franklin permission to accompany me to Spain as a war correspondent, fearing he may engage in bullfighting, twelve thousand Italian troops were landed at Malaga and Cadiz. . . . "

Now enters another villain of the Spanish Civil War— Communism. Stalin helped the Loyalists. His aid was doled out with an eye-dropper perhaps, but nevertheless, he put Russia solidly on the side of the established, Republican government, which had no place else to turn.

Whatever his long range motives—and the motives of Stalin were always devious—he nevertheless saw clearly that this struggle in unhappy Spain was just the opener in a war in which the Axis would eventually embroil the whole world. By enabling the Republic to resist Franco and his German-Italian allies he felt perhaps that Russia's example would be followed by the democracies and that the larger catastrophe could be avoided. Eventually, too late, and to their great sorrow, the democracies saw what he had meant.

[135]

The word went out. Anti-Fascists everywhere took up the hint. Along with a high percentage of Communists, they joined up in the so-called International Brigades.

The Russian aid, and the gallantry of the Brigade undoubtedly helped the government to hold-out as long as it did. Their blind dedication, the obedience, the disciplined iron-hard will, plus the courage of the Spanish themselves kept the fight going in the face of what came to be overwhelming odds.

This was the situation that caused anyone who upheld the Republican side, as Hemingway did, to be accused of the taint of Communism. All Loyalists were "known" to be Communists, to be "Red." Anyone who fought in Spain with the Loyalists had borne arms with Communists, had associated with them freely, and thus had assisted them in their devious scheming. Hemingway was not exempt from these charges. Many times the color of his political flag was questioned. He answers the accusations with a flat: "I had no Stalinist period."

He was no wool-gathering, dreamy idealist getting cozy with Communists because of sympathy with their political philosophy. Quite the contrary. As always, he saw things clearly, the way they really were. The Republic had been thrown, not through choice, into Stalin's arms. Hemingway was completely realistic and he so acted. If Communists could help beat the Fascists and save the Republic, he would fight with them. This was Hemingway's position, and it was the position of the United States much later during World War II.

Hemingway stuck by his guns. During the conflict and after it, he never wavered in his belief in the Spanish Republic and the Spanish people. In 1959, he told a group of Catholic

[*136*]

school children: "I had seen the Republic start. I was there when King Alfonso left and I watched the people write their constitution. That was the last Republic that had started in Europe and I believed in it. I believe the Republican side could have won the war and there would have been an okay Republic in Spain today. Everybody mixed into that war. But knowing Spaniards I believe the Republic would have gotten rid of all the non-Spaniards when the war was over. They don't want any other people trying to run them."

In February of 1937, Hemingway left for Spain.

Among the Loyalists he found an electric air of excitement and confidence. Their troops had just celebrated a great victory over the Italian at Brihuega. Visiting the battlefield, Hemingway could not help but feel a great surge of joy. But he also felt enormous compassion and pity, the legend of his bloodthirstiness notwithstanding. In spite of the Loyalist propaganda, in spite of his own hatred of Mussolini, he was compelled to observe that these Italian poor men's sons had died bravely, victims of superior firepower, air attacks, inadequate protection. As he looked at the shattered bodies, they did not seem to be Fascists, nor devils. They were just dead men, sons, possibly, of brave men he had fought with along the Piave nearly 20 years before.

This was the "golden period," if ever there was one, in the war. This was the time when he thought the Loyalists would win. This was the brief time of unity and cohesion in the Republic. It was the time of glory of the International Brigades, of hope, of good comradeship. Politics had started the war but it played no part now in the lives of Hemingway and his companions. These companions were of all political colors—from outright Reds clear around the circle to Hemingway's position—that of an artist, an American, and a staunch supporter of the Spanish Republic.

Aside from his activities as a correspondent, Hemingway joined in the war effort in all ways and manners, most of them dangerous, illegal, and unofficial. He drilled young Spaniards in the arts of war, of guerilla fighting, in the use of the rifle and machine gun.

He assisted in the production of a documentary propaganda film, "The Spanish Earth," with John dos Passos, Lillian Hellman, Archibald MacLeish, and other prominent Americans. Highly indicative of the *real* character of Hemingway is the fact that just at this moment, when he was freely giving his time and money in the production of this film, he turned down an offer of $4,500 a week to write movie scripts in Hollywood. In making "The Spanish Earth," he might well have lost his life. The "sets" were the battlefields. Daily, he guided camera crew and the director, a young Dutchman, Joris Ivens, to film actual combat—tank battles, infantry attacks, patrol sorties, machine-gun duels.

Hemingway made the 12th International Brigade, commanded by a Hungarian, General Matel Lukacs, his "home' outfit. Lukacs was an intelligent, gay and joyous companion. Among his other close friends were the medical officer, Werner Heilbrun, and Gustav Regler, one of the most able fighting officers in the Brigade. This was the truly "Republican" Brigade, and closest to Hemingway's heart. Also from time to time he visited the 11th International Brigade, composed mostly of Germans—ardent anti-Nazis. "Most of them were Commu-

Hemingway saw his beloved Spain plowed in the furrows of war.

nists," he says, and "a little too serious to spend much time with."

By May 19, 1937, Hemingway was once more back in the United States editing and putting in the sound track on "The Spanish Earth." It was shown in the White House for President and Mrs. Roosevelt. Subsequent showings throughout the country brought in thousands of dollars to the Loyalist cause.

In 1934, Hemingway had published in *Cosmopolitan* a long story called "One Trip Across." a "socially significant" story about a proud and independent man, Harry Morgan. Morgan took to smuggling from Cuba rather than let himself and his wife go on relief during the depression. A second story about Harry Morgan had appeared in *Esquire* in 1935.

These two stories, plus additional material he was to add, became the basis of a new novel. At first glance the idea seemed a good one. He planned to finish the book during this first trip home to America from Spain. Because of many pressures, however, the book was not coming to life. There was no time available for the necessary rewriting. His heart was not in it—all his thoughts and energies were directed across the water to Spain.

Nevertheless, he continued to tinker with the book when he could, and after he hastily went over the galley sheets, it was finally published. This was Hemingway's only deliberate excursion into the world of "social justice" writing, which was just as well. The book was not a good one in spite of the fact that it contains some very fine writing. Possibly with more time and fewer distractions, Hemingway could have made *To Have and Have Not* vastly better.

During this period at home, the Hemingway legend, if indeed by now it needed any additional fuel, was further stoked by an encounter with Max Eastman, a critic. In an article Eastman had written some things which Hemingway considered insulting. Among them was the accusation that he wore "false hair" on his chest, meaning of course, that he was a big bluff.

The two men met quite by chance in Maxwell Perkins' office at Scribner's. The legend-makers had a field day. Hemingway was a boxer, Eastman allegedly a wrestler. Soon, the stories go, they were slugging it out. Desks were supposed to have been overturned, chairs smashed, papers scattered about.

After the "battle" was over, Hemingway went with friends to a showing of "The Spanish Earth." When they emerged from the theater, the news was out. White-faced with fury, but helpless to repair the damage, Hemingway read the headlines: EASTMAN KO'S HEMINGWAY!!!

What had really happened? Hemingway spoke his piece to Eastman, then shoved the offending book in his face. Eastman's "nose-print" on the page remained to prove the point. Then he departed. And this was all. Again, the truth had been magnified all out of proportion. A silly scuffle had been distorted beyond recognition.

Three days after the row, on August 14, 1937, "false hair" on his chest waving belligerently, he took off for the indisputably bloody and dangerous tragedy of Spain.

Papa, as Hemingway was by now universally called— affectionately or derisively, depending upon the point of view— found things vastly different than on his first trip.

The old companions were gone. Lukacs and Heilbrun were both dead and buried. Regler, desperately wounded by a

pound and a half of steel that uncovered his kidneys and spi-
nal cord, lived to be put in a French concentration camp.

Madrid was a bitter snarl of dissension and cynicism. The
stern and disciplined Communists were taking over more and
more. Gone was the lighthearted will to victory. Desperation
took its place. The International Brigades hadn't lost any of
their effectiveness as fighting units, but they were now quarreling
and fighting among themselves. These Brigades were composed
of men of extremely diverse political leanings. Now, in the face
of increasing Communist power, they were less and less in-
clined to submerge their own political and religious affiliations
in the greater overall need of the Spanish Republic.

Also, Italian and German troops and supplies were flood-
ing into Spain. The war became a test-tube war, with the Fascist commanders unleashing for trial against the helpless Spanish people all their latest devilish contraptions. Squadrons of
powerful tanks maneuvered and tried out new tactics. New
types of flamethrowers seared the earth. The most efficient mod-
els of high speed machine guns, pistols, quick-firing field cannon, and anti-aircraft guns were given a thorough testing. The
Luftwaffe came into its own and learned new lessons in the
art of bombing troops as well as defenceless cities. Machine-
gunning civilians and refugees was also a new technique and
had to be perfected. The pilots had lots of practice.

The siege of Madrid tightened. At the Hotel Florida where
Hemingway lived, a choice of different cuts of horsemeat was
offered on the menu. The misery of the population increased
as the city more and more became a mass of rubble.

In his hotel, to the accompaniment of bursting artillery
shells, Hemingway wrote his only play, *The Fifth Column*. It

contained some very fine writing, but as a whole, was not a very good play. Perhaps, like *To Have and Have Not,* it would have been better had it been written under conditions a little less harrowing.

Its artistic merits aside, the play naturally infuriated the Rebels. While sympathetic to the Loyalists, it also was harshly attacked by them! It did not, they said, portray the nobility and the grandeur of the Spanish soul and spirit and the Loyalist cause. The real trouble probably was that even in times as trying as these, Hemingway was a writer before he was a partisan. The play not only showed that war, any war, "is hell," but it also stated that more often than not it is waged by fanatics who become demons and ultimately bear little resemblance to human beings. Hemingway's first obligation as he saw it, as always, was to tell what he considered to be the turth.

The truth was that by now Spain and its predicament was a hopeless tangle of politics, loyalties, religion—on both sides. The war staggered on in a bath of blood and hatred such as the world has seldom seen. Brother fought against brother, priest against priest, family against family. In a rising crescendo of horror the ferocity grew and took life of its own, destroying everything in its path.

Besides writing, and drilling troops, it is difficult to find out for sure what else Hemingway did during these bitter days. The legend says one thing: He carried ammunition and manned field guns. He mixed Molotov cocktails, bottles filled with gasoline set afire with a cloth wick, and hurled them with imprecations at advancing Fascist tanks. He stuck by his chattering machine guns until the barrels melted and ran at his feet! And so on. Papa always had a good public.

[*143*]

Some things he *did* do. He made impassioned speeches to Republican troops who were fighting among themselves. He helped recover the shattered bodies of victims buried in rubble during the bombardments. He acted as a father to small children whose own fathers had been killed. He helped in the makeshift hospitals, trying to ease the wounded. Most of all, because of what he was, he observed and missed nothing. "I'm going to write about this," he said, "after the war is over. I'm going to *try* to write about it."

Twenty-five years later, thinking of these terrible days, he wrote, "I had quit praying for myself during the Spanish Civil War, when I saw the terrible things that happened to other people and I felt that to pray for one's self was selfish and egotistical."

He returned to the United States in January, 1938, and went back again in March. Stoutly he insisted to the public that the Loyalists would win but he did feel privately that the cause was doomed. Too much German-Italian materiel and too many men—all on the wrong side—had poured into the country. Fifth columns were at work in most of the cities and the people of Madrid and the whole Republic were starving. Furthermore, Hemingway was too acute an observer of the international scene. He could only go on hoping against hope, but the drift of the world was toward the appeasement of the Fascists, toward the crowning debacle at Munich. Spain was caught inexorably in this drift, far too much so for Hemingway to have entertained more than a wan hope that she could survive. But he wasn't about to give up hope or admit defeat while his Spanish friends were still dying.

Papa was back in America again by June 1, but he could

not rest so long as there was a shred of Loyalist resistance. He returned to Spain in September and stayed all through the gloomy and heartbreaking days of the final collapse. He never ceased believing in the Loyalist cause. When the end finally came, he escaped over the mountains into France in March, 1939.

Thirteen years later he returned to Spain. He had been assured that it was safe for him to do so. All his friends on both sides were out of jail. Also, a bull had been dedicated to him, which must have meant that he was once again "respectable" in the eyes of the Franco government.

He wrote, "It was strange going back to Spain again. I had never expected to be allowed to return to the country that I loved more than any other except my own . . ."

Hemingway never set himself up in the "prophet business." It is surprising, though, how many of the things he has said have come true. These statements were not prophecies in the sense in which we ordinarily think of such things. They were more like simple comments made by an extraordinarily clear-sighted man.

In 1938 he wrote in a small pamphlet, along with a good many other famous people, a commentary on Milton Wolff, the ninth commander of the American Abraham Lincoln Brigade (four were dead and four badly wounded): "He is a retired major now at twenty-three and still alive and pretty soon he will be coming home as other men his rank and age came home after the peace at Appomattox courthouse long ago. Except the peace was made at Munich now and no good men will be at home for long."

Hemingway wrote a novel about the Spanish Civil War, *For Whom the Bell Tolls,* the favorite of many readers. The story is very simple. It is that of Robert Jordan, an American volunteer in Spain, who joins a group of guerillas ordered to blow up a bridge.

If the story is simple, and the time span it covers is short, the book is neither. It is very many things—including practically a textbook on guerilla warfare, a diatribe against war, and a philosophical discourse on the basic needs for survival—food, shelter, clothing, and courage.

It is not a "political" novel. It is a novel about people in a highly political scene. Hemingway takes the opportunity to clarify once and for all his own position regarding Spanish politics. Steadfastly, he, through Jordan, disclaims political affiliations. He had none. He seems to be seeking a faith but mistrusts them all. "He accepted their discipline [the Communists'] for the duration of the war because, in the conduct of the war, they were the only party whose program he could respect." The book finally is a study in pure human tragedy.

Hemingway took 18 months of sweat and labor to write *For Whom the Bell Tolls.* Some of the work was done in Key West, some in the corner room at the Hotel Ambos Mundos in Havana. He pondered long over each part of it. He wrote and rewrote. Into it he put, so he says not just the Civil War "but everything I had learned about Spain for eighteen years."

When the book came out it pleased nobody except the public! Millions of people bought it. It became one of the great all time best sellers. Over 1,000,000 copies in English alone were sold. The movies paid him $150,000 for the rights to film it. Naturally the book enraged the Franco government of

Spain. In Hemingway's acceptance of the Republic, they saw him as a pure Red Stalinist.

Also, the book infuriated Communists all over the world. Hemingway had, they claimed, been unfair and unjust in drawing scenes representing Red commissars as ruthless, mean, heartless, or cynical, or for even hinting that the Loyalist government had ever wavered or seemed confused about its course. It even incensed veterans of the Lincoln Brigade as the American who fought in Spain named their unit. Hemingway had retreated. He had gone soft. He had betrayed them. They even carped because Jordan, in the book, slept in a sleeping bag! There'd been no such amenities in the Spain where they had fought. Hemingway just didn't understand the war at all!

Hemingway rode out the storms. He'd written the truth as he'd seen it, as a fine writer in search of the truth. This was enough for him.

The war in Spain had been Act I of a tragedy that soon was to sear the world. Now, in Europe, the curtain was rising on Act II.

But meantime, Hemingway had his own problems.

Chapter 10

The Third Time Around

Like a good many men before and after him, Hemingway had considerable trouble with women.

In his writing, he seems to have had difficulty casting his women properly for the part he chose for them to play. Almost without exception the plots of his books and stories radiate outward from a core of strong, virile masculinity. As his characters move and tug about this center, there are of course, women among them.

The feeling is inescapable, however, that once he brought women into such a story plot, he didn't exactly know what to do with them. They're beautiful, they're ugly, they're noble, or they're demons—whatever the situation requires—but somehow, they just don't become human! The reader has the feeling that Hemingway is uncomfortable with his heroines. He senses that something about them he doesn't understand makes him uneasy.

Hemingway was an acute observer. He was a master at putting down what he observed and bringing it to life. There is no difficulty in *seeing* his women. But they're drawn so well that they seem to take on an existence all their own. They become independent, they get away from the writer and turn into something unlike what he had in mind. Perhaps he oversentimentalized them, overromanticized them. In the face of such treatment, they rebelled.

In real life too, Papa had the same problem. He never had a daughter; if he had had perhaps he would have seen the opposite sex a little more realistically. This longing for a female child was deep rooted. As time went on he gave up hope, but never his illusion about what she might have been. His son John says, "In Papa's language, any pleasing female person is called 'Daughter,' regardless of age." Marlene Dietrich, nearly his own age, was such a case. He was enormously fond of her, and she of him. He invariable called her "daughter."

He tended to put his wives in roles that were impossible for any flesh and blood woman to play. His own rugged maleness seemed to demand as a foil the kind of woman who no longer existed—if that type *ever* existed. Those dear, sweet, girls who could be all things to a man were pure fiction.

Privately, and in some bitterness, Pauline remarked to friends that the Spanish Civil War had cost her both her husband and her faith. This very well may be true. Ernest was away from home a great deal, passionately devoting his time and his energy to things she could not share. Furthermore, Pauline was a devout Catholic; when Hemingway married her he had been converted to Catholicism. All the religious angles, cross-currents of suspicion and lack of understanding and sympathy that arose out of the conflict tore and shook both of them very deeply.

Hemingway was capable of extremely deep love and loyalty. But sometimes outside pressures can be too strong even for this. Though he tried hard to save this marriage, it was no use. They were divorced in 1940.

Seventeen days after the divorce, Papa was married again. The new Mrs. Hemingway was Martha Gelhorn, a beautiful foreign correspondent he'd met in Spain.

Papa apparently couldn't live with women, nor could he live without them. He'd married Pauline only three weeks after his divorce from Hadley. When he fell in love he fell hard, like a big oak crashing to the ground. He always married the girls he loved—right away. And they loved him. After the initial bitterness of the divorces were over, they had nothing but good to say about Papa. All except Martha Gelhorn, who, when her turn came, said nothing. She wasn't going to comment publicly on such a personal matter!

Martha was exceptionally beautiful, and intelligent. She was also a very good writer. They went to China on their honeymoon, to report on the war there. Martha's luggage consisted mainly of her typewriter and a traveling bag, field glasses, hiking boots, and flannel trousers. She also packed one evening dress, but somewhat apologetically. "I doubt that there'll be many formal affairs to go to in Chungking." The honeymoon over, they returned to live in Cuba. Martha shared with Papa a great love of everything Latin. He bought a 15 acre estate outside Havana and here they settled down in an atmosphere of books, writing, swimming, fishing, endless house guests, and considerable drinking!

The name of the estate was *Finca Vigia,* which means watchtower, or lookout farm. It took its name from a beautiful old house that had at one time actually been used as a lookout tower.

Hemingway wrote in one room of the tower with a pencil. Martha banged away in another on her typewriter. Everything seemed very cozy and chummy.

Troubles soon arose. Nobody knows exactly what happened. Martha wasn't the talking kind. The chances are that her ceaseless writing became a kind of literary competition that began to get under Papa's skin. By 1944 the marriage was in serious trouble. He'd decided that never again would he marry a writer. His next wife—and the last—Mary Welsh, was also a writer, but when she married Papa she very wisely gave up her career.

In 1940, when Martha and Papa came to live at *Finca Vigia*, Act II of the holocaust called World War II was already under way in Europe and the dark clouds were shadowing America as well.

Papa was tired. He'd been on the go for years. He needed a holiday, he needed to rest, to think, to relax, to try to evaluate what he'd seen. He took time off. He fished on the beloved *Pilar*. He went to fights. He took an interest in cockfighting and raised his own birds. He read. He enjoyed the steady stream of guests of every color and description. He drank in the Havana bars.

And then came Pearl Harbor on December 7, 1941. By this time Papa was again ready and raring to go.

He joined the United States Navy. He joined it as a ready-made captain, doing the thing he loved to do—fishing. Papa persuaded the powers that be that the *Pilar* would make the finest Q-boat they'd ever had in the service. Q-boats were disguised as commercial vessels in order to lure enemy submarines into firing range.

During the early days of the war, Nazi submarines had a field day in the Caribbean. It was choked with shipping bound through the Panama Canal to and from all the widely scattered battle fronts. The smoke from burning tankers and freighters almost daily smudged the clear tropic sky. United States authorities lived in mortal fear that the vital Canal itself would be attacked and destroyed.

The bays and inlets of the Latin American mainland, and the countless islands, many of them completely uninhabited, made it difficult to track down the U-boats. Spies, saboteurs, and fifth column traitors were landed without hindrance from submarines. They refueled and picked up food and ammunition from previously arranged depots on the islands or from carefully disguised supply ships.

The gleaming, polished *Pilar* was turned into a warship. Bunks were installed for nine crewmen. Larger fuel tanks, larger water tanks and a greater storage capacity for food made her capable of long, offshore cruises. She was also loaded to the railings with the tools of war. In her armament there were rifles, machine guns, pistols, grenades, bazookas, high explosives. She was also equipped with high power radio.

For a while she was even armored! Heavy steel plate was secured fore and aft. Papa discarded it after a bit. It slowed her too much and also pulled her down by the head. The chances were too great that in a seaway running full speed she might have nosed into a swell and turned herself permanently into a submarine.

Spruille Braden, the United States Ambassador to Cuba at the time, was something of a daredevil in his own right and approved of Papa's idea completely and enthusiastically.

Hemingway knew the Caribbean as well as he knew the top of the desk at which he wrote. He knew the likely spots where U-boats might refuel; he knew the probable routes they would take to make rendevous with supply ships. He planned to bag one!

Even armed as she was, the *Pilar* was no match for a submarine. One torpedo would have blown her to splinters. But Papa had a plan. It was pretty farfetched but it might have worked—knowing Papa. He and the crew would masquerade as simple sports fishermen in carefully chosen areas. He hoped that eventually a submarine would surface and order him to come alongside. What would happen then was anybody's guess, but apparently there were two battle plans. In one he would aim the *Pilar* right at the sub and ram it. The impact would set off the high explosives aboard the *Pilar* and blow everything, including the submarine to bits. Just before impact the crew of the *Pilar* was to dive overboard and presumably be saved. The other plan of action called for the *Pilar* to come alongside the submarine. At the propitious moment Papa was to lob a carefully prepared bundle of dynamite into the conning tower.

The plan might have worked, only it never had a chance to be tried out. The *Pilar* never made contact with the enemy. Papa located a number of subs, even saw the thin trailing lines of periscopes looking them over. The information he radioed back is credited with enabling the Navy patrol bombers to make several kills. And this is as close as he got.

By 1944 he was fed up with his terrible fisherman's luck. About all he had to show for his pains was a very beatup

Pilar, and an irritating, itching skin from the long hours under the sun. Because it hurt him to shave, he grew a beard—the famous beard that was from then on to be a Hemingway trademark.

Hemingway donned the uniform of a war correspondent, went to work for *Collier's* (Martha was already covering the Mediterranean front for the same magazine), and headed for Europe.

Now the Hemingway legend really came to life. How it grew! And the strange part is that during these crazy, action-filled months in Europe, no embellishment was necessary. It is hard to sort out fact from fable in this confused time, but the truth seems to be even wilder than any fable.

Everything started calmly enough. Papa arrived in London and immediately began flying with RAF bombing missions over Germany. Pretty dull stuff. Nothing happened at all and he just sweated out the time until D-day, when he could get in some action on the ground.

Of course, Papa got hurt! He usually managed somehow to add to his collection of scars. Everything was most prosaic. While riding in a car during the night in blacked-out London, he received a bad head wound in an accident. The concussion was severe enough, but Papa was used to them by now. His great fear was that they would not let him out of the hospital in time to join the Normandy invasion. He was cheered, however, when the doctors told him "that that part of his brain he used to write with wasn't damaged."

Also during this time in London he met Mary Welsh, who was later to become his fourth and last wife. She was, like

[*155*]

Martha, a journalist, being currently a correspondent for *Time*.

Whether he made it for D-day or not lacks authentification. One report has him in on the first wave. Another says he scrambled ashore on the third. Still another claims he didn't actually get to France until way into July, more than a month after the invasion. When he got there he made up for lost time.

Possibly there has never been as unenthusiastic a reporter as the European correspondent for *Collier's!* He filed something like six stories during the whole time he was overseas, just enough to keep him from being fired and sent home. Papa hadn't come to this war to write. He'd come to fight and he'd never felt better about it. Old time opponents, the Fascists and Nazis, were his enemies and he went after them.

Officially he was assigned to General Patton's Third Army. He didn't like the job with its requirement of sending lengthy weekly dispatches back home. Also, he did not like General Patton. One can't help thinking that possibly Patton, a very fine soldier, was just as virile, just as flamboyant, and just as aware of his "public" as Hemingway. They rubbed each other the wrong way.

Hemingway left the Third Army and "attached" himself to the Fourth Infantry Division of the First Army. Here he found good companionship and fewer restrictions. After the breakthrough at St. Lo, Papa was off and running.

He "appointed" himself a captain, commandeered a jeep. He loaded it with arms, ammunition, and cognac. With his helmet perched on top of his still bandaged head, and with his beard whistling in the wind like an old time buccaneer, he set sail for the German lines.

Guerilla warfare was Papa's meat. He was an expert at it.

Sixty miles behind the lines he began recruiting his own private army of French underground fighters. Soon he had well over 200 men in his "army." They were as ragged and nondescript a group as could every hope to be seen. They were also as deadly a gang as ever made a bomb in a kitchen. They were armed to the teeth and they were fighters. Not the least of them in armament or in fighting ability was commander Hemingway.

Hemingway knew war. He'd fought in two of them and in the interim had studied their conduct backwards and forwards. He'd kept his hand in too by hunting large and small game of all kinds with weapons of every description.

His men adored their "general" and followed him blindly, but there was one fly in the ointment. They could not understand why such a warrior, a man of such advanced age, a man with so many honorable wounds, a man so skilled in the arts of war with so much obvious service, could only be a captain. Why had he not advanced further in rank? His men were a little embarrassed for him and in the presence of strangers, usually addressed him as "colonel."

But they were upset about it, and finally Papa let them in on the secret. "Young man," he said to one of his *maquis* who questioned him, "I have not been able to advance in rank due to the fact that I cannot read or write." His men clucked their tongues in pity, but it didn't really matter. Their "illiterate" commanding officer knew his business and that was all that counted.

When the Americans finally entered St. Michel they found a battered sign on the cathedral: "Property of Ernest Hemingway." This was only the start. Word began drifting back about the exploits. He tossed hand grenades into a cellar where

Nazi panzer soldiers were hiding. He sat calmly through a meal in the kitchen of a farmhouse he had requisitioned as head-quarters. When everybody dived for cover during a shelling Papa continued to eat his omelet and wash it down with huge gulps of wine. He directed the emplacement of machine guns to provide cross fire and then, flat on his stomach, was nearly buried in leaves as enemy fire snipped off branches just inches above him. He sat tranquilly, all night long, at peace with him-self if not the world, with a submachine gun in his lap and grenades clustered like grapes about his middle, to give his companions a chance to sleep.

There were many, many such incidents. He maneuvered his "army" back and forth, to the right and to the left, haras-sing the Gemans and upsetting their communications. One of his principal activities was gathering information which he sent back to the more slowly advancing Allied armies, with their more cautious commanders!

His jeep and his men kept appearing at the most unlikely places. General Raymond O. Barton, commander of the Fourth Division, recalled that as he briefed other, more orthodox cor-respondents on the progress of the war, he "always kept a pin in the map for old Ernie Hemingway. He's sending back in-formation. But now what do you think he says? He says that if he's going to hold out where he is, he'll need tanks!"

Papa's great ambition was to get to Paris, his early love. The Allies had decided that a French armored column, under General Le Clerc, should be the first to enter the city. Le Clerc was a stiff officer of the old school. He didn't go much on correspondents, nor on irregulars in general. Nevertheless, the intelligence sent by Hemingway regarding the disposition of German troops cut in half the time it took Le Clerc to reach the city.

But Papa was already there! He'd taken back roads known to himself and his men and as Le Clerc maneuvered cautiously outside of town, the Hemingway irregulars fought a battle with the Germans under the Arc de Triomphe.

In a way, you might say that Papa captured Paris.

His first act was to look up old friends. With Hemingway at the head in his jeep, his column swung sturdily along behind him, bellowing a marching song that had always been a favorite of their commander. It went like this:

Dix bis Avenue des Gobelins,
Dix BIS AVENUE des Gobelins,
DIX BIS AVENUES DES Gobelins,
THAT'S WHERE BY BUMBY LIVES!

Such memories. It was the little verse he had taught the infant Bumby so many years ago to help the youngster find his way home if ever he became lost. And now Papa was home.

He stopped at the studio of his old friend Picasso. When he found that the painter was all right he left him, but only after presenting the gentle man with a load of hand grenades just in case. His next stop was on the Rue de l'Odéon, at Sylvia Beach's Shakespeare Book Shop. Here as a young man he'd received mail and he'd done a lot of reading, rubbing shoulders with the great—Joyce, Pound, Dos Passos, and many others.

Sylvia wrote: "There was still a lot of shooting going on . . . and we were tired of it when one day a string of jeeps

[*159*]

Papa came back to Paris in triumph.

. . . stopped in front of my house. I heard a deep voice calling 'Sylvia.' And everybody in the street took up the cry, 'Sylvia!' "

She rushed downstairs, met Papa with a crash. "He picked me up and swung me around and kissed me while people on the street and in the windows cheered. He was in battle dress, grimy and bloody. A machine gun clanked on the floor.

Sylvia got him a bar of soap and after he had cleaned up, he asked, "Is there anything we can do for you?"

"Yes, Nazi snipers on the roof are bothering us."

Hemingway took some of his men up on the roof, there

[*160*]

was some firing, and that was the last of it.

Papa rode off grandly, so he said, "to liberate the cellar of the Ritz."

When Robert Capa, the famous photographer and buddy of Hemingway's during some of the guerilla forays, finally arrived much later, Papa's driver was on guard at the door. "You go up quick," he said. "Plenty good stuff in the cellar."

The wild, incoherent days of the occupation of Paris were over at last and the Allies ground on toward Berlin. Papa as usual was in the van. But at last he was stopped. He came bang up against the Siegfried line. Even he had to sit on his haunches and await reinforcements from the slowpoke armies behind him.

But he'd also run into another wall more formidable than the Siegfried Line. Task Force Hemingway finally met its equal in deviousness and rock-hard dedication: The Legal Department of the Inspector General's Office of the United States Army.

They said war was a matter for *professional* soldiers, not amateurs. Furthermore the rules of the Geneva Convention state that war correspondents are not to carry arms. Pencils, not machine guns are their weapons. They are not to command troops.

As Hemingway fought his way through the Hurtgen Forest and all the other bloody battles after Paris and as he was figuring out a way to assault personally the Siegfried Line, the lawyers investigated. They finally concluded that Papa should testify himself. He reported back to Paris after first carefully getting rid of such evidence as guns, grenades, and the like.

The interrogation dragged on. He was saved only by the

testimony of fellow correspondents and other friends. None of them, it soon appeared, had *ever* seen Big Ernie commanding soldiers or carrying arms of any kind whatsover! The investigation was finally closed. The lawyers couldn't find the evidence. Investigation disclosed "no violation by him of the existing regulations for war correspondents." Little wonder. His soldiers worshipped him. The Inquisition itself could not have made them alter their testimony.

Instead of bringing him up for disciplinary action, eventually, much, much later, they got around to awarding him the Bronze Star. The citation reads "for valor and for superior intelligence reporting." Papa had put in a lot of time and taken a lot of risks in his day fighting for what he believed to be right. He had earned the decoration.

For the occasion of its presentation, he even shaved off his beard. The picture is one of the few taken in which he is not grinning. His face is humble and deadly serious. Later he was to tell his friend Colonel C. T. "Buck" Lanham, destined to become the prototype for a character in a future book: "In the next war I'm going to have the Geneva Convention tattooed on my backside in reverse, so I can read it with a mirror." It's easy enough to imagine the broad grin on Papa's face when he said this.

This had been a big war. He'd believed in it. He said, "Most of this last war made sense, while the first one made little sense to me. . . . Also, it was the first time I ever had a chance to fight in my own language." His only regret was that he hadn't been first into Berlin to confront the Führer with his sins. Perhaps this would have been a little too much to ask, even for Ernest Hemingway.

By now, Papa was *really* tired. He needed to rest. His big body was worn out. The scars, the wounds, the emotional battles of a lifetime, culminating in the War, had taken a heavy toll, greater than he had realized. He was ready to call it quits for a while and settle down. For the first time in his life his mind and powerful frame were in rebellion at the ceaseless indignities and abuses he had heaped upon them.

But before he could rest, there was one more distasteful job that had to be done. His marriage with Martha was on the rocks. With as little fuss as possible for a man of his prominence, he got a quick Havana divorce in December, 1945.

He had loved three women truly, with all his heart, but something always went wrong. He'd lost all three of them. Permanent happiness with a woman didn't seem to be in the deck for Ernest Hemingway. Here is how he put it, through the mouth of one of his fictional characters, a weary old soldier: "I have loved but three women and have lost them thrice. You lose them the same way you lose a battalion; by errors of judgment; orders that are impossible to fulfill, and through impossible conditions. Also through brutality."

Thus Papa indicted himself.

At this dark and despairing moment, another woman walked into his life. She was blonde, petite Mary Welsh, the *Time* correspondent he'd met in London. They were married in Havana early in 1946. She was just what he needed and as it turned out, Mary, or Miss Mary as he lovingly called her, was truly to be his enduring love.

They settled down at *Finca Vigia,* where Papa could lick his wounds, rest, think—and get back to his own trade.

Chapter 11

The Center of the World

In a certain way Hemingway had enjoyed the action, the danger, the excitement and masculine companionship of the war. He was also proud of the part he had played in bringing final victory.

But he was also a sensitive man. His own philosophy had steadied him. Personally he was not afraid of death. He knew that each man owed God a death; that a man could die but once and that this inevitable end must be shared by all men, by all living things. What other men could endure, so could he.

He was also sickened, however. The mass bloodletting and killing was brutalizing. Such a thundering tragedy of suffering was a degrading thing. At *Finca Vigia* he began to mend, but slowly.

Hemingway was 47 years old when he and Mary settled in Cuba. His health was not very good. The physical and emotional scars were deep. But gradually, under the healing sun, being with people he loved, doing the things he liked, he once more began to embrace life.

He did as he wished to do. He lived as he wished to live. He struggled constantly to live a life of truth, the only kind of an existence in which he could believe. Without sham, without hypocrisy, without lies of any kind. This is endeavor enough for any man.

The next thirteen years were possibly the happiest time of Papa's life. This was a joyous, golden time, of work and of love.

Why did he live in Cuba? He answered the question himself in an article in *Holiday* in 1949: " . . . it is because you like it. It is too complicated to explain about the early morning in the hills above Havana where every morning is cool and fresh on the hottest day in summer. There is no need to tell them that one reason . . . is because you can raise your own fighting cocks. . . .

"You do not tell them about the strange and lovely birds that are on the farm the year around . . . nor that quail come in the early mornings to drink at the swimming pool, nor about the different types of lizards that live and hunt in the thatched arbor. . . . You do not try to explain about our ball team—hard ball—where, if you are over forty, you can have a boy run for you. . . .

"You could tell them that you live in Cuba because you only have to put shoes on when you come into town, and that you can plug the bell in the party-line telephone with paper . . . and that you work as well there in those cool early mornings as you ever have worked anywhere in the world. But those are professional secrets."

The simple things, the joyous things were loved by Papa, and he saw and appreciated them all. Cuba was the center of their world. From it he branched out in every direction. And to it the world streamed in on him—good and bad, the great and the small, old friends and new, and strangers.

If Cuba was the center of the world, at *its* center was the tranquil haven of the *Finca.* It was on a small hilltop, a part of the village, and yet separated by thick growth from it. Its curtains were stirred and the soft yellow tilework cooled by alternate breezes from land and sea. One was heavy with the lulling and abiding fragrance of the earth. The other sharp with the exciting and heady scent of the ocean. One could walk and dream along secluded paths. There was a big swimming pool, a tennis court, a space to set up an impromptu ring for boxing.

At *Finca Vigia,* the years passed in lovely disorder, filled to the brim with work and the pleasures dearest to his heart. At first the seclusion was nearly complete, but as time went by, the visitors poured in. Papa enjoyed them. He was the soul of hospitality and was never happier than when holding "court." At times though, it got to be too much. He put up "No Trespassing" signs and finally a fence, but it was useless. The old Hemingway magic was at work, and people—invited and uninvited—knocked on the door. *Finca Vigia* was the center of the world; and besides, when had Papa ever protested overly at a good time, a good argument, a lively sparring match?

And so the people came—writers and would-be writers, college professors, critics, boxers, ball players, bullfighters, actresses, escapees from Devil's Island, priests who'd fought with the Loyalists in the Spanish war. The list was endless.

There were but two rigid requirements. The early hours of the morning were sacred for work. Guests and family alike must go on tiptoe. And, whether the visitors were men or women, they had to be human beings interested in what they were doing and good at it. No phonies, please.

[*167*]

The famous beard turned to salt and pepper to iron grey and finally to snow white. With his ample girth and broad, grinning face, he had the appearance of something between a Santa Claus and a venerable lion. He was truly Papa now. A kind of rough and ready "father" to all who climbed the little hill to the tower. A father with all the answers—except perhaps to those of his own questions.

He was full of the old devil himself, but his health was still not so good as he might have wished. He tired easily. He put on far more weight than was good for him. There were rumblings of discontent in his liver. The steady drinking did little to calm the vague portents of more serious problems. And Papa was weary, more worn than he knew. But life was still very good.

Action and fun and fishing and lots of talk filled the days, especially the talk. The subjects ranged from the sublime to the comic, and all the way back again.

What did art mean? Anybody's art? Papa's art?

What had been the real meaning to the world of the Spanish Civil War. How had people been so blind?

Who could throw the hardest punch in the crowd? Only one way to find out. The Dodgers were in training in Havana and some of them took up the challenge in the big living room. Gloves were donned and before you could say "farewell to arms," bottles were crashing, furniture was overturned.

Miss Mary rushed into the room, screaming for the fight to stop. Papa at the moment was recovering his poise from a prone position on the floor. He rose slowly to his feet, grinning. "That's all right, honey," he said. "We're just having a little fun."

[*168*]

Who likes lion steaks? Miss Mary described them as delicious—tender and succulent—a real table delicacy. Before anybody knew what was happening, uncomplimentary remarks about her and her tastes were printed in the Havana papers. Papa took objection to them, the columnist was insulted, challenges flew thick and fast. In the resulting melee of words, Papa refused to his credit to become involved in a duel with loaded pistols over lion steaks!

During these years, Papa's sons—Bumby, Patrick, and the youngest whom they called Gigi—were frequent visitors. They were indeed chips off the old block.

Bumby had been with the OSS in the war. When dropped by parachute back of the German lines, he had been captured. Papa had been all for organizing an immediate commando raid but Bumby managed his release by himself!

They all loved hunting and fishing with a passion equal to their father's. His former wife Pauline once complained to a friend in Seattle that while she shared their love for steelhead fishing, "she was getting too old for this sleeping bag stuff on the ground in the mountains!"

Several times they organized a trout fly tying business, and to Papa's disgust, with only indifferent success! They had better luck with guns. They were all crack shots; Patrick, the middle son, later became a white hunter in Kenya.

Little Gigi developed a magic eye with a shotgun. Papa spent long hours coaching him at *Finca Vigia,* and the other boys turned this ability to their considerable advantage. Pigeon shooting was a popular sport in Cuba and they entered Gigi in the competitive matches at the swank gun club in Havana. After passing the word around that their rather unprepossessing

[169]

looking little brother was no great shakes with a shotgun, they proceeded to place large bets on him. They cleaned up until the local betting circles wised up!

So it went. There was never a dull moment on the farm, which was just the way the bearded patriarch of the hilltop liked it.

Sometimes the volume of uninvited guests—"the jerks and the twerps, the creeps and the squares and the drips . . . [who] seem, with the new antibiotics, to have attained a sort of creeping immortality"—grew so great that there was nothing to be done but flee. Or maybe this was just an excuse. Papa had always been a great one for getting about.

For normal emergencies, the beloved *Pilar* offered ready sanctuary. Nearly every afternoon, when the day's work was done, she put to sea. Papa, and soon Miss Mary also, was never happier than with three or four baited lines riding the wake, a full lunch basket, and plenty of beer on ice in the galley.

There were close shaves. Papa hadn't gotten over his habit of getting hurt. Once, in a heavy seaway coming in to the anchorage, he slipped and cracked his head open. He was out like a stone with a bad concussion and a spurting cut artery. He nearly bled to death before they could get to a surgeon and have him stitched up.

On another trip to Venice while duck shooting, disaster again nearly overtook him. A piece of wadding from a shotgun shell went in an eye. Eye injuries were so common he'd long since ignored them. This one became infected however and according to friends, it took 16,000,000 units of penicillin to save his life! While in the hospital at Padua he worked out in his mind and actually started to work on another book.

In 1953 Miss Mary and Hemingway were traveling in Africa. While acting as a deputy game warden in Kenya, Papa left off hunting a leopard that had been decimating native goat herds to deliver a Christmas present to Miss Mary. She wanted a plane ride over the headwaters of the Nile. In a light Cessna 180 they took in the various points of interest, including Murchison Falls. While they were looking over the stupendous 400 foot drop, a flock of ibis rose into the air. To avoid ploughing through the birds, the pilot crash landed in a clump of trees. Hemingway and the pilot were unhurt, but Miss Mary suffered two broken ribs.

They spent the night in the forest, right in the middle of a herd of elephants. Hemingway said, "An elephant prowled around our camp for about two hours. Several times he was only twelve feet away. He looked like a moving mountain in the moonlight. He seemed to listen more attentively to my wife's loud snoring. When we woke her up, she said, "I never snore. That is just one of your ideas."

"Obviously the elephant had the same idea," countered her husband.

Eventually a launch came by, one of those little, iron hulled steam boats, like the one used on location by the movie company when they filmed the "African Queen." In its venerable, slow way, it putt-putted the trio to civilization.

Meantime the whole world was alerted and a vast search by land and air was underway. The wrecked plane was found, but no survivors. It was assumed that old "accident prone Papa" had finally met his end.

Eventually the three survivors reached a place called Butiaba, in Uganda. Here they met one of the search planes and the pilot offered to fly them to the nearest large city. In taking off, this plane crashed! Simply unbelievable! The plane burned, but again everyone escaped alive. Hemingway, however, was very badly hurt.

The legend now took over and stated that Papa, roaring belligerence like a wounded lion, with a bottle of gin in one hand and a stalk of bananas over one shoulder, made his way finally back to civilization. While lying in the hospital, he had the rare pleasure of reading his own obituaries. Most of them laid great emphasis on the fact that he had sought death all his life and now had encountered it.

He snorted. "Can one imagine that if a man sought death all of his life he could not have found her before the age of fifty-four? It is one thing to be in the proximity of death, to know more or less what she is, and it is quite another thing to seek her. She is the most easy thing to find that I know of. . . . There are so many ways of finding her that it is stupid to enumerate them."

Eventually he and Miss Mary were well. They pasted the obituaries in a zebra skin bound scrap book and returned to *Finca Vigia.*

If *Finca Vigia* was the center about which Papa's life revolved in these years, *it* also had a beloved center—his wife. For the first time he was fully happy with a woman. He loved Miss Mary more deeply than he had ever loved before. His love for her was greater than the drive of his own blistering ego. In this love he could submerge the problems and the agonies and find real peace. She was at last the symbol of womanhood come to life which he had carried in his heart for so long. She was his bridge, as every man believes his ideal woman to be, between earth and heaven.

She showed her love in a thousand ways. At *Finca Vigia,* on the *Pilar,* while traveling. She managed to love him the way he wanted to be loved and in so doing, she took happiness and grace upon herself. She understood his problems. She knew how tortured he was inside and forgave if he blustered, if he drank too much, if he was difficult. She knew that in the *real* Papa, inside the rough, often abrasive exterior, there was greatness—greatness and real gentleness. Most of the happiness and the tranquillity of these later years of his life he owed to Miss Mary, and he never ceased to recognize it, and to sing her virtues.

As Papa played, as he lived hard, as he wandered, hunted, fished, as he growled his way through the pitfalls and mountains of the public legend, what about this man inside?

The writer? What about the work that gave him impetus and direction and meaning? What of the ecstasy and the torment? The cantina in the Hotel Ambos Mundos in Havana is dark and cool. It is a quiet masculine retreat of mahogany, amarillo wood, and mirrors. In a secluded corner is a stool. This stool was the private perch of *El Senor* Ernest Hemingway. From this stool he could see in the mirrors who was coming in from the hot brilliance outside. From this stool he ruled, and was petted and pampered. Never was his glass dry; never was the snack dish empty of the bits of *seviche*—raw fish steeped in lime and lemon juice and pepper—of the tiny dried shrimps and other delicacies he loved. Papa spent much time here.

When everything was going well and the typewriter, or the pencil, had turned out its daily quota, Papa's bar chits ran to $20 or $30 a day! Yes, he wrote because he had to, he wrote so he could live and his friends could live and enjoy life with him.

But Papa knew his big problem. It was that bar stool! Like a good general planning a campaign, he carefully laid out the terrain on which the battle would be fought.

The *Pilar* was berthed not at Havana, but at Cojimar, 27 miles way. In between Cojimar and Havana lay home, *Finca Vigia*. This made it difficult—just pleasantly so—to get to the *Pilar* for the afternoon's fishing. This also made it difficult—slightly more so—for him to wind up at the end of the day on the stool at the cantina. When visitors overran the farm to the point where he had to get away to work, he moved for awhile into the old corner room in the hotel. When this happened, the bar stool became more a problem.

But in spite of the bar stool, in spite of the visitors, the hunting, the fishing, the visitors, the traveling, all the accidents, the fine instrument of Papa's talent was not allowed to lie idle. He said, "In going where you have to go and doing what you have to do, and seeing what you have to see, you dull and blunt the instrument you write with. But I would rather have it bent and dulled and know I had to put it to the grindstone again and hammer it into shape and put a whetstone to it, and know that I had something to write about, than to have it bright and shining and nothing to say, or smooth and well-oiled in the closet, but unused . . . . it is necessary to get to the grindstone. . . . I would like to live long enough to write three more novels and twenty-five more stories. I know some pretty good ones."

Hemingway's crown was secure as just about America's

greatest writer. Like all champs, he defended his title. He put his nose, and his talent, to the grindstone. He wrote steadily.

The critics who liked him continued to like him. Those who didn't continued to snipe away. Papa had never taken adverse criticism easily; and these days, if anything, he became even more sensitive, more enraged at those who accused him of every crime under the literary sun.

In the meantime, enraged or not, he did the thing he knew how to do. He wrote, sometimes in the room at the hotel, sometimes in sickbeds or hospital rooms, most often in the windswept study on the fourth floor of the tower-like house at the farm. As the years advanced, the steps up to the top seemed steeper and longer. His legs were weary and the huge body was tired. Finally he surrendered and moved his study down to the bottom floor. These days he had to write standing up. Pain in his legs and back made it impossible for him to sit over long periods.

He wrote as he had always written—about life as he saw it. He strove always for the essence of truth, for the vision in words of things as they really were. He gave the best that was in him. He wrote as good writers always write—as though each word were going to be his last.

In these years many magazines —*Life, Look, Esquire,* and others—were more than glad to publish him.

There were also books. In 1950 the book that was an outgrowth of World War II, the one he had started in the hospital in Italy while he had been recovering from the shotgun wadding eye wound, came out. He called it *Across the River and Into the Trees.* The book was written fast—at white heat. Hemingway was ill during much of its writing and felt it necessary to get it off his chest as quickly as possible.

The novel was a love story, told almost as the summation of a weary, old soldier's life. The reviews were mixed but for the most part unflattering. Possibly the critics were right in this case. The book was written too fast. The War had not yet had time to jell and to distill itself into the essence that was so imperative in order for Hemingway to see clearly. In addition, there was the usual hue and cry that the girl was unreal. They said she was his usual symbol, the dream girl who never came to life.

Way back in 1936 Hemingway had written an essay for *Esquire*. He called it "On the Blue Water (A Gulf Stream Letter)." The story told of an old fisherman who had all alone hooked a gigantic marlin. While the old man attempted to tow the huge fish back to land, it had been devoured by sharks. This was the germ of the story—actually it was a novelette— that he entitled *The Old Man and the Sea*. *Life* published the entire story in one issue in 1952.

Those who loved Hemingway's work were lavish in their praise. The story they said was filled with beauty, truth, mysticism, and symbolic meaning. Those who didn't like him pointed to it as just another example of his dedication to a rough and ready and meaningless code of ethics and conduct. Only time will tell whether it is the brightest jewel in his crown or not. One thing however, is sure. *The Old Man and the Sea* contains some of his finest writing: unadorned and direct yet tremendously beautiful and evocative in its severe simplicity.

Of all that Ernest Hemingway has, or has not, contributed to the world as a writer, one thing is certain: he has given the English-speaking world a new look at its language. He has managed to put down on paper words as they are spoken, as they are thought, by living people. He has cut through the bombast, the clichés, the flowery unreal phrasing that makes so much other writing only a distorted shadow of English as it is actually used. He gave it simplicity; he gave it honesty. He stripped meanings of their gloss and of falsity so that they ring true to eyes and ears. Possibly this very quality is what has earned for him the reputation of callousness, of being the apostle of violence. This is not correct. It is the honesty that shines through. If we insist on finding violence and brutality in his simple words then we must admit that we ourselves are violent and brutal. And this is not so. It is hard to look honestly at ourselves; he forces us to do so by the elimination of trivia.

Because of his vast knowledge of the sea and of fishing, Papa assisted in the preparation of the film of *The Old Man and the Sea*. One of his tasks was to provide the action sequences in which the giant marlin was hooked. Alas for his famed angling ability! In spite of a long trip even to the far-off waters of Peru, he was never able to catch the monster that they needed.

For all the controversy over *The Old Man and the Sea,* it won Papa the Pulitzer prize in 1953. He sent the $500 check to his son John, then an Army captain stationed at Fort Bragg. He added in a note "It is the same as five months' jump pay."

When word came of the awarding of the prize Papa was at sea in the *Pilar* riding out a blow. The radio was tuned to the weather reports when he learned the news. "I was glad," he said, "I was not at home so as not to say anything wrong on the telephone. . . . I am going to watch my——mouth now

[*177*]

for a couple of years and see what happens. Maybe I will get respectable. Wouldn't that be wonderful."

The same year, Papa had also been under consideration for a Nobel Prize in literature. But in 1953, the prize was given to Winston Churchill. By 1954, however, the Swedish committee evidently decided they had better not put Papa off any longer. An official explained: "He was due to receive the award eventually, and we might as well give it to him now before he kills himself in some adventure."

The official news came over the Cuban radio on October 28, 1954, and *Finca Vigia* was of course swamped by letters, calls, telegrams, and newspapermen. Papa received a medal, a scroll, and $36,000. The last was especially welcome. Living was on a big scale at the farm and expenses were high. The "goose that laid all the golden eggs" was, according to him, often short of money. At the time the award was made Papa claimed he was $8,000 in debt.

Because Papa was suffering from injuries at the time, his doctor would not let him go to Stockholm for the ceremonies. He said, "As a Nobel prize winner I cannot but regret that the award was never given to Mark Twain, nor to Henry James speaking only of my countrymen. Greater writers than these also did not receive the prize. I would have been happy—happier—today if the prize had gone to . . . Isak Dinesen, or to Bernard Berenson . . . [or] to Carl Sandburg. . . . [But] I should not make any such observation. Anyone receiving an honor must receive it in humility."

And in his acceptance message he spoke from the heart of what was really inside him. ". . . Organizations for writers palliate the writers' loneliness, but I doubt if they improve his writing. . . .

"For a true writer, each book should be a new beginning where he tries again for something that is beyond attainment. He should always try for something that has never been done or that others have tried and failed."

And so Papa kept writing. He never stopped. Many of his works had been published. Many other manuscrips, as yet unpublished, were in safe-deposit boxes and vaults for safe-keeping. Perhaps some day they'll see the light.

By the late 1950's, shadows were closing down about Papa and Miss Mary and the lovely sun-lit life at *Finca Vigia.*

Cuba could use a good revolution, he once said. When Castro staged his revolt, like so many other people, Papa welcomed it. But time had not dimmed his perception; he soon saw that the way *this* revolution was going would make it impossible for him to continue to live in Cuba. As he'd once said long ago when referring to Fascists, this time he might once again have said, ". . . a writer who will not lie cannot live and work in a country run by bullies . . ."

In addition to his increasing dissatisfaction with the politics of Cuba and his fear of what he knew must be coming, Papa's health was also failing. He was by now really ill.

His eyesight was bad. He'd gone through very serious liver trouble. He had put on far too much weight. His heart was acting up: high blood pressure with all its problems had overtaken him. Emotionally he was exhausted, worn out. Insomnia wracked him night after night. The hot, sea-level climate of Cuba was barely tolerable.

Those last seven years since the plane crashes in Africa seemed almost a period of decline. Reluctantly he and Miss

Mary faced up to what must have been one of the most difficult decisions two people had ever confronted. They must leave the center of their world. They must leave *Finca Vigia,* the simple people in the village, the *Pilar,* the bar stool in the Ambos Mundos, their pool, the shady walks swept by the trade winds, the gardens. The whole fabric of their lives had to be torn up.

For a new home they chose Ketchum, Idaho, near Sun Valley. The altitude was right, the climate was good, and the hunting was fine in the valleys and uplands of the mountains.

In 1959, when Papa was 60, they were settled in their new home.

Chapter 12

Endings

The burnished Spanish sky flowed out of immense distances to cover the earth. Beneath the blue, from horizon to horizon, stretched the yellow and brown and ochre of the land. The town reared up out of the earth. It was alien. It seemed to intrude rather than to nestle in the curve of hills.

Late afternoon sun streamed down into the Plaza de Toros. It flooded the bullring with hard light, glinted from the horns of the bull, glittered dully along his bulging shoulders, the enormous black flanks.

The bull glared at the matador with wary eyes. Tamed and brought to bay, he wearily dug the sand with his hooves . . . and he watched and waited.

Gently, rhythmically, Antonio Ordoñez moved in closer. His body was coiled, tensed. The long blade was poised. Suddenly he arched forward, standing high on his toes. The sword gleamed and then slipped deep between the massive shoulder muscles of the bull.

The bull shuddered as though at the face of some horror he had seen. Then he dropped to his knees and fell to the earth.

Papa at last got back to the Spanish bullrings he loved.

Ernest Hemingway, huge, was hunched in a ringside seat. He relaxed, gazed somberly at the slender, deadly matador, his "suit of lights" glittering. Then his glance moved slowly to the massive dead animal before him. Hemingway nodded, murmured to himself. Neither the man nor the beast had failed. The bull had fought his fight with courage. When the end had come inevitably, he had faced his death with dignity. The man had bestowed it with grace and sure strength.

"Perhaps," he mused, "the gift of death is the greatest of all gifts . . . to receive or to bestow. The final test for him who receives it and him who gives it."

The heat of the day was lifting. People streamed from the bullring into the streets of the town and were grateful for the cool of evening.

On a bench along one wall of a café, a guitarist probed

[*182*]

the strings gently with searching fingers. Beside him a dancer clapped softly, tentatively reaching for the rhythm of flamenco. The cafe was crowded; more people arrived every moment.

At a table Ordoñez and Hemingway sat with a bottle of wine between them. The air crackled with Spanish, with excited comments on the afternoon. Men greeted the matador with great respect.

They saluted Hemingway with deep affection.

"Hola, Papa."

"Que tal, Papa?"

"Papa Ernesto, buenas tardes."

As the men called him by name, to each he lifted his glass in greeting. These were his people; to their affection he returned his love.

Hemingway finally looked across the table to Ordoñez. He grinned, lifted the glass again. "And to you also, Tonio. The bulls were very beautiful and brave this afternoon."

Ordoñez smiled, *"Como siempre,"* he murmured as he drank. The tension was fast draining from him. "Yes," he nodded, "the bulls were fast and courageous. They knew how to live . . . and they knew how to die. What more can one ask?"

They were silent a moment, then Ordoñez laughed broadly. "You know, Don Ernesto, the Swedish radio reports *your* death. Here in Spain, this afternoon."

Papa roared with laughter, his face quivering inside the snowy halo of beard. *"Que pendejada.* Such foolishness. Spain is a country to live in, not die."

Ordoñez nodded, smiled, but his dark eyes were thoughtful. These were the eyes of a man who looked often upon

[*183*]

death, a man who often administered it. They were trained eyes and they didn't miss now the tremble in Hemingway's fingers nor the indefinable look in the face, of watchful waiting . . .

Ordoñez twirled the wine glass. "Papa," he said softly, "have you made your plans for next year?"

Hemingway nodded. "Yes. I'll see you at the fiesta in Pamplona in July. And then we shall make the fighting circuit together . . . as I used to do with your father."

The late fall sky of Idaho was taut and glittering. It spilled thin light down on the little town of Ketchum. It bathed the jagged mountains and the deep valleys with yellow glow. Mid afternoon. The school children were out and ran shouting through the streets.

Those who passed in front of Ernest Hemingway's house all slowed to talk a moment. To them he was nothing of the great man. He was Papa.

"Hello, Papa."

"How are you today, Papa?"

Their voices rang in the golden air. His greeting to them was always the same, warm and courteous, without the tones of impatience or condescension so often heard in the greetings of adults to children.

"Hello, child," he'd say. Occasionally his hand went out to rumple the hair of a shy little girl or to give a boy a vigorous dutch rub.

A little boy, about ten years old, passed by. He was thin, wiry, and sunburned. His face and his eyes had that pinched, faraway look that boys invariably have when they spend much

[*184*]

time outdoors and the mountains and horizons are distant. He carried a gun, a .22 rifle that had been a very special present to him from Hemingway.

"Let's go hunting today, Papa."

"Not today, child." The flick of disappointment on the boy's face was not missed by Hemingway, and so he was quick to add. "You're old enough to go by yourself. Remember what I told you about a fine bead and be sure to allow for windage. Bring me a rabbit."

"You bet. Or maybe a couple of squirrels. But I'd rather go with you."

The boy ran off and in the eye of his mind Hemingway followed him along the country roads and the trails in the woods, through land he loved, wonderful, eternal land. Then he turned and slowly went into his backyard. For the rest of the afternoon he shot clay pigeons, the pop of his shotgun soft in the clear air.

That evening Hemingway settled in front of the television set to watch the Motion Picture Academy Awards from Hollywood. Jimmy Stewart accepted a special Oscar for Gary Cooper, who was unable to attend. As he took the little statuette, tears came to Stewart's eyes and he was unable to control his voice. This was the first that Hemingway, or the country as a whole, had known of the gravity of Cooper's illness.

Cooper and Papa were old, old friends. Cooper had acted in films made from Hemingway's work. Their admiration for each other had grown and often they hunted together.

Hemingway immediately went to the phone and called the hospital in Beverly Hills.

Pale and weak, dying of cancer, Cooper took the call in

his bed. It was good to hear his old friend's voice.

"Hello Coop, you old so and so. How are you?"

"Not so good, Ernest."

There was a long pause, then Hemingway said, "I'm sick too, Coop."

"I bet I'll beat you to the barn, Papa," said Cooper.

Slowly Hemingway returned the phone to its cradle.

He was sick. The decline had speeded alarmingly. Now, in the fall of 1960, he was swiftly failing.

The great body was reduced and wasted. The muscles of his neck, the tremendous arms and shoulders, were drooping, uncertain of their movements. Worse, this seemed more than a physical decline. The searching, "interested" eyes seemed to have lost some of their eagerness. Visitors reported that the fierce spirit that had attacked and embraced life with such gusto had softened. He seemed to be tamed, brought to bay, mortally wounded.

His local physician, Dr. Saviers, had been treating Hemingway for hypertension, that is, high blood pressure. By the end of November, 1960, his condition was so bad that it required special attention. Accordingly, he entered the Mayo Clinic in Rochester, Minnesota. He registered under the name of Dr. Saviers.

The visit to the Mayo Clinic turned into a 53-day ordeal. He was treated for hypertension. He was treated for incipient diabetes. He was found still to be suffering from liver trouble.

But mostly, Papa, now barely 60 years old, was suffering from a lifetime of injuries and abuses. His body was worn out. The endless wounds in battles, wars, hunting, airplane accidents, concussions, boxing, fighting, brawling, drinking had finally caught up with him. He had not only written about life, he had lived it hard, clear to the limit. Only an iron constitution could have survived so many years.

When he returned to Ketchum from the Clinic, he was restricted in his diet, his drink, his exercise, his hunting. He could no longer even trapshoot. One thing he could do, however: he could write. He never surrendered. He wrote and wrote. He conducted himself like a champion. He did what he knew how to do and never gave up.

All his working life, the last thing Hemingway had done at the end of each day was to count the words he had written. This running word-count had been his daily progress report for more years than he could remember. And now, in addition to the word-count, he charted his daily weight! Thus there were now checked two vital statistics: a slowly and painfully mounting total of words and a slowly and painfully dwindling body weight.

By April of 1961, his condition had again worsened. He was in misery, depressed. The blood pressure climbed steadily; his body hurt. Soon he was back in the Mayo Clinic again—this time under his own name. The whole world knew now that Papa was really sick. The reservations to meet Antonio Ordoñez in Pamplona for the fiesta had sadly to be cancelled.

Two months later he was again discharged from the hospital. With George Brown, a very old friend and a sparring partner from happier days, he started back home. Miss Mary drove very slowly. They took five days for the drive through the hot summer.

The heat haze was misty on the hills back of the house and quail called to each other in the underbrush when they

[*187*]

arrived home. Papa was tired, more than a little glad to be back.

That evening Papa, George, and Miss Mary dined at a favorite restaurant in nearby Sun Valley. The meal was pleasant and relaxed. Later, preparing for bed, Miss Mary walked across the hallway to Papa's bedroom. He was in the bathroom, brushing his teeth.

She said, "I have a present for you." She began to sing an old Italian song. Neither of them had thought of it for years. *Tutti Mi Chiamano Bionda* it was called—Everybody Tells Me I'm a Blonde!

Hemingway listened as she sang and then, grinning, joined in the last verse. He sang a bit off-key, as usual.

Miss Mary looked at her husband closely as she told him goodnight. The siege in the hospital had been difficult; the trip home had been hard. Then she kissed him and went to her room.

He sighed deeply as he put out his light and settled for the night.

Bitter insominia wracked him. The nights no longer were made for love, or sleep, or laughter. Now they were only for thinking . . . and for the futility of remembering . . . and for loneliness.

Hemingway had written at the time of receiving the Nobel Prize: "Writing, at its best, is a lonely life . . . he [the writer] grows in public stature as he sheds his loneliness and often his work deteriorates. For he does his work alone and if he is a good enough writer he must face eternity, or the lack of it each day. . . . It is because we have had such great writers in the past that a writer is driven far out past where he can go, out to where no one can help him."

He thrashed wearily . . . "to face eternity . . . or the lack of it each day . . . *out to where no one can help him* . . ."

Outside a night bird hooted over the valley as it winged in the darkness toward the mountains. The wind was cool at this altitude, but fresh and sweet. It carried the scent of the abiding earth, which he had always loved, into the room. The abiding earth, to which all things must return.

Next morning about seven thirty, Miss Mary was awakened by a shot from downstairs. When she got to the living room, Papa was dead, killed by a blast from a shotgun.

Had it been suicide? How easy to say that it was!

To quote his son John . . . Bumby . . . ". . . if you have guns or anything else you like very much, you pick them up. You should be careful with them, but Papa was in *very* bad shape. So, there *is* a question of doubt, no matter what anybody may feel. There *is* doubt."

And to quote finally, from Ernest Hemingway himself . . . ". . . the job is to *understand, not judge.*"

All mortals return to dust . . . even giants. Individuals die but the sweet earth abides forever, just as life itself is eternal and forever rises again. Just as surely as the sun also rises . . .

EPILOGUE

Years ago Archibald MacLeish, a famous poet and critic, wrote in a poem about Hemingway:

> . . . the lad in the Rue de Notre Dame des Champs
> In the carpenter's loft on the left-hand side going down—
> The lad with the supple look like a sleepy panther—
> And what became of him? Fame became of him.
> Veteran out of the wars before he was twenty:
> Famous at twenty-five: thirty a master—
> Whittled a style for his time from a walnut stick
> In a carpenter's loft in a street of that April city.

"What became of Hemingway? Fame became of him, yes, but something more, I think, than fame. Art became of him—became of him in the truest and the largest sense. Rilke once said of the writing of a verse: it is not enough merely to feel; one must also see and touch and know. But it is not enough either, to see and touch and know: one must have memories of love and pain and death. But not even these memories are enough; the memories must be "turned to blood within us" so that they are no longer distinguishable from ourselves. Experience, Rilke was declaring, must turn into man before a poem can be written. Experience, that is to say, must reach such an intensity that it contains our own being. When that happens —when experience and man *so* meet—the poem may be written and when the poem is written we may discover who we are.

Hemingway brought himself to face experience of this intensity not once, but more than once. And what became of him was that great triumph."

ACKNOWLEDGEMENT

To Jay Allen I am extremely grateful. It is impossible to discharge the enormous debt of gratitude I owe him for many long hours of discussion, for his patience in going over the manuscript, and for the additional insights he has given me. In part payment, many thanks.

Paul Rink